Google™ Apps
Administrator Guide

David W. Boles

THOMSON

COURSE TECHNOLOGY

Professional ■ Technical ■ Reference

Important: Thomson Course Technology PTR cannot provide software support. Please contact the appropriate software manufacturer's technical support line or Web site for assistance.

Thomson Course Technology PTR and the author have attempted throughout this book to distinguish proprietary trademarks from descriptive terms by following the capitalization style used by the manufacturer.

Information contained in this book has been obtained by Thomson Course Technology PTR from sources believed to be reliable. However, because of the possibility of human or mechanical error by our sources, Thomson Course Technology PTR, or others, the Publisher does not guarantee the accuracy, adequacy, or completeness of any information and is not responsible for any errors or omissions or the results obtained from use of such information. Readers should be particularly aware of the fact that the Internet is an ever-changing entity. Some facts may have changed since this book went to press.

Educational facilities, companies, and organizations interested in multiple copies or licensing of this book should contact the Publisher for quantity discount information. Training manuals, CD-ROMs, and portions of this book are also available individually or can be tailored for specific needs.

ISBN-10: 1-59863-451-8
ISBN-13: 978-1-59863-451-8

Library of Congress Catalog Card Number: 2007931837

Printed in the United States of America

08 09 10 11 12 TW 10 9 8 7 6 5 4 3 2 1

THOMSON

★ ™

COURSE TECHNOLOGY

Professional ■ Technical ■ Reference

Thomson Course Technology PTR, a division of Thomson Learning Inc.
25 Thomson Place
Boston, MA 02210
http://www.courseptr.com

Publisher and General Manager, Thomson Course Technology PTR:
Stacy L. Hiquet

Associate Director of Marketing:
Sarah O'Donnell

Manager of Editorial Services:
Heather Talbot

Marketing Manager:
Mark Hughes

Executive Editor:
Kevin Harreld

Project/Copy Editor:
Kezia Endsley

Technical Reviewer:
Gordon Davidescu

PTR Editorial Services Coordinator:
Erin Johnson

Interior Layout Tech:
Value Chain, Ltd.

Cover Designer:
Mike Tanamachi

Indexer:
Katherine Stimson

Proofreader:
Gene Redding

This book is dedicated to my beloved wife Janna Marie Sweenie, who for over 20 years has stood shoulder-to-shoulder and heartbeat-to-heartbeat with me.

Acknowledgments

Big thanks to SuperAgent Matt Wagner of Fresh Books, who is always reliable in friendship, persistent in negotiation, and insightful in the marketplace. I am grateful to Kevin Harreld at Course Technology PTR for having the vision to see the value of *Google Apps Administrator Guide* long before it came into being. I appreciate the keen eye and kind hand of my editor, Kezia Endsley, who always made everything you read here better. Thank you also to Gordon Davidescu, who provided a careful and spot-on technical edit. Thanks, too, to all the behind-the-scenes Super-Geniuses at Thomson whom I have yet to meet, but who have already given us their finest work, including Gene Redding and Katherine Stimson. I also want to express my respect for the readers of my Urban Semiotic blog–you always provide outstanding feedback and criticism for all my writing efforts. The tidings for this book began with your comments. I also thank Google–and my secret Google insiders–for their advice and for creating such fine software that can handle both celebrating and poking without losing a single stride. Finally, a slew of kudos go to the faculty, staff, and student body of Boles University, who all know in their bones if it isn't happening online, it isn't happening at all.

About the Author

David W. Boles currently hails from the urban Heights of Jersey City, New Jersey, after finding birth on the hard, crackling, plains of the Nebraska prairie. Other books include GIS material for three textbooks from Glencoe/McGraw-Hill, *Hand Jive: American Sign Language for*

Real Life–with Janna M. Sweenie–for Barnes & Noble Publishing New York, and *Windows 95 Communication and Online Secrets* for IDG Books Worldwide. *Bad Baby Signs: Words No Infant Should Know!* is a new project, providing a laughing look at the ever-expanding Baby Signs Movement, and is co-written with Janna M. Sweenie. David has written for c|net, boot, and *Windows Magazine* and was a writer for and the East Coast Editor of *eyepiece* — the official publication of the Guild of British Camera Technicians.

David's MFA is from Columbia University. His polymathic teaching credits range from Public Health to Technical Theatre to Playwriting, Directing, Composition, Criticism, and American Sign Language and include fine institutions of higher learning such as Columbia University, New York University, Fordham University, University of Medicine and Dentistry of New Jersey, New Jersey Institute of Technology, Rutgers University, Saint Peter's College, and the College of New Rochelle. He served as a visiting professor at the UC Davis program in Sports Medicine. He is also the founder of *Urban Semiotic*, a blog examining the hardships of living poor in the city core. David is the founder of Boles University, located locally online at http://BolesUniversity.com.

Table of Contents

Introduction

Welcome! You don't have to be a computer geek or an Internet genius to use this book. In fact, if you're just starting out with domain hosting and email and want to take the quick but safe route to using Google Apps, this is the right book for you.

Together we will step through all pinnacles of the service while stepping over the pitfalls that have already struck the virgin unwitting. I made many mistakes setting up my domain, and as your personal Google Apps "pro," I will share with you my wisdom so you won't repeat the errors I made. I have already done all the dirty work for you.

Google Apps is perfect for schools, businesses, families, and organizations. You don't have to be rich or a *Fortune* 500 company to take advantage of its fine features. In fact, you can get most of the Google Apps service entirely free if you don't need tons of email storage space and guaranteed email uptime. We'll figure out which version of Google Apps is right for you in Chapter 2.

The main Web site for *Google Apps Administrator Guide* is located online at http://BolesBooks.com/thomson/, and you can always find the latest information on the book at that site. Because Google Apps is always in flux, I have decided to protect your purchase of this book with online updates and bonus chapters that will include any and all major changes to Google Apps that occur between the time I finish writing the book and the time the book hits the bookstores. Visiting http://BolesBooks.com/thomson/ often will ensure you always have the latest Google Apps information.

The online bonus chapters for *Google Apps Administrator Guide* are available only to those who purchased this book. You need a username and password to ensure that only those who bought *Google Apps Administrator Guide* can access the updated information and bonus chapters. Check online at http://BolesBooks.com/thomson/ for simple instructions on accessing the protected content.

Google Apps has a rich, if brief, history of successes, and the beautiful part of that is this: You benefit from those who came and conquered before you, and you are using the exact same bandwidth, service, and Google machines as the big boys. That's a tempting offer of excellence you can accept and enjoy throughout this book.

Let's get started!

1 Your Google Apps Introduction

Google Apps will soon take over your life and the lives of others.

You know that already because you were smart enough and keen enough and prescient enough to buy this *Google Apps Administrator Guide*, and so you have a bell curve lead over others who pretend to know where the Web is going and how we'll all work together and collaborate with each other online in the virtual cloud some of us call "The Google," where everything is known, and everyone is controlled by you know who.

I'm Kidding; But Not Really

Okay, so maybe I'm kidding about Google taking over the world—but you know better. You know Google is the perpetual king of search, and that sort of scalable power and divination from database mining is invaluable.

With Google watching your back and hosting your apps online via its service, you are buying a bet into the future of the Internet that we will move away from the home computer box for our high-powered collaborations, and the Web browser will become the key to unlocking our lives with each other as we spread our connections and internetworking across the world while fuzzing international boundaries and local guideposts.

The Serious Beauty; No Kidding

The beautiful thing about Google Apps is the simple beauty of the interface. When you understand how the calendar works, you already understand how to add new users and share documents and put up a few blog pages.

The universality of Google Apps in function and comprehension is built into the design of the experience. This book you hold in your non-virtual hands will step you through the process of setting up your domain and getting your users online and active.

The power of Google Apps is that it provides you total, customizable, complete control over your users, email (Gmail), a private label start page, documents, spreadsheets and presentations, Blogger, Google Talk, Google Calendar, and Google Page Creator. I will work through all of those features and get them set up for you in the pages of this book.

Pretty Platform Independent

Google Apps is platform independent. It doesn't matter if you like to use Windows or a Mac or Linux or a cellular phone or some other odd operating system. Google Apps works and lives beyond the immediate you on Google servers across the world.

All you need is an Internet connection and a good, up-to-date Web browser, and you are ready to set up and manage your domain with Google Apps.

How Will This Book Help You?

You don't have to be a computer geek or an Internet genius to use this book. In fact, if you're just starting out with domain hosting and email and want to take the quick, but safe, route to using Google Apps, this is the right book for you.

Together we will step through all pinnacles of the service while stepping over the pitfalls that have already struck the virgin unwitting. I made many mistakes setting up my domain, and as your personal Google Apps "pro," I will share with you my wisdom so you won't repeat the errors I made. I have already done all the dirty work for you.

Google Apps is perfect for schools, businesses, families, and organizations. You don't have to be rich or a *Fortune* 500 company to take advantage of its fine features. In fact, you can get most of the Google Apps service entirely free if you don't need tons of email storage space and guaranteed email uptime. We'll figure out which version of Google Apps is right for you in Chapter 2.

Easy Enough for a Nine-Year-Old

This book is for you–the new Google Apps domain administrator–if you seek an easy-to-read guide for getting your domain online and setting it up to work with Google Apps.

If you are a nine-year-old with an Internet connection, a browser, and access to a domain zone file, you can set up and administer a Google Apps domain. It's just that easy.

If you are older than a nine-year-old, I know the process of working with Google Apps will be even more fruitful for you–mainly because you won't have to spend so much time asking Mom and Dad for your turn to use the computer.

A Taste Test: Picking One of Semi-Four Flavors

Google Apps currently comes in four "flavors." This book will cover all four flavor implementations, and we'll discuss the choices more in depth in Chapter 2. Here's a quick taste of the four options:

* Education Edition: You need to have a pre-existing .EDU domain. If you don't understand what that means or how you get an .EDU domain assigned to you, the Education flavor is not available to you as an administrator.

* Standard Edition: This is the most popular version because it is free and you can add lots of users. There are a few downsides–because you get what you pay for–and if you aren't paying, there are some guarantees you will miss.

* Premier Edition: You currently pay $50.00 USD per user if you want the Premier flavor of Google Apps. There are reasons for paying Google for Google Apps–because you get what you pay for–and for some of us, paying around $4.00 USD a month for a guaranteed, advertising-free service is worth every single penny in the bargain.

* Nonprofit Edition: Google recently added a semi-fourth flavor of Google Apps for nonprofits in the United States, and this program is an extension of the Education Edition of Google Apps. If you operate a registered nonprofit, the Nonprofit Education Edition is a fine program for your organization. This edition includes little or no upfront investment because everything is free, and full technical support from Google is included in the bargain!

No matter which of the four Google Apps flavors you choose, I can help you get that edition up and working because that is the beauty and the purpose of this book.

A Brief History of a Googleteer

Sometimes you pick up a computer book and read the introduction, and you are left with a cold and sterile feeling. You might wonder aloud before the purchase, "Is this author into the software or not?" I think magnitude and passion are important in writing and in effective communication. You have the right to know up front if your author is a fraud or a fanboy, and I can tell you from direct experience that a fanboy is more fun to read.

I consider myself a temperate Google fanboy–a "Googleteer," if you will–because for many years, my life has inexplicably–okay, by choice–pretty much revolved around the Google sun in my research and writing on the Web.

It is difficult to escape the prick of the Google hook as it pierces the meaty part of your fingers and mind during a simple Web search by providing you precisely the link to the wonder you seek. Google is the king of Internet data for a reason: They know all about your wants and needs, and they remember where you've been and why you went there.

I first came to Google several years ago via its search engine. I became a fully formed Googleteer in 2004 when I read about a newfangled "Google mail" service called Gmail that launched on April Fool's

Day. The official Google announcement can be seen at http://www.google.com/press/pressrel/gmail.html

If you weren't lucky enough to get a Gmail invitation to the beta testing, you had to go underground and into the black market to pay someone to give you an invitation. That meant going on eBay and bidding to buy a Gmail beta invite.

I bit and paid $40.00 USD in an instant "Buy Now" purchase so I could have Gmail, the username I wanted, and Gmail's astonishing 2 gigabytes of email storage space.

Once you had a Gmail beta account, you could either turn around and sell and invite–and even though it was against Google's Terms of Service, everyone was doing it at the time; I privately think Google loved the aping and the "I'll pay to play" appeal of the beta test–or you could be nice and offer your friends a beta test invite for Gmail for free.

The fact that Gmail is still in beta is a curiosity, but I suppose Google can protect its interests by excusing any problems with the service by saying, "You get what you pay for, and we're still in beta three years later..."

I did not sell any of my beta invites. I offered them to my university faculty colleagues and students in my class. All the students went wild and took me up on my offer.

None of the faculty wanted an account because they felt Google was violating their privacy by placing Adsense advertising next to their mail. The faculty did not like the idea that "Google was reading their email." What they failed to realize was that their spam blocker was "reading" their mail with the same intention and purpose as Google: to sort and show certain email in a predetermined context.

I tell you that story about Gmail and old-timer concern about new technology because you, as a Google Apps domain administrator, might face the same sort of resistance when moving your email and calendars and such into the Google cloud. People might express concerns with privacy and reliability and availability of services. Some might not completely like or understand the notion of labeling messages in a giant pool of information instead of segregating them in separate folders. I will help you learn how to frame your answers in a context that will soothe any pending concerns from those above you in the chain of command and those below whom you are required to serve with kindness and aplomb.

A Semiotic Promise

I am a big believer in teaching via memes and semiotics–universal ideas and images–because it is always better to share and show and not tell. I promise you whenever possible I will lead you through the Google Apps learning curve by using common terms as well as screenshot images that will show you precisely what steps to take.

Books are formed by text and given definition by their images. We are fortunate that computer books place an equal value in both the word and the eye and, by honoring both sides of the brain, we will operate on all learning levels over the experience of this book.

Those Who Have Come Before You

We find great value in the effort of those who have blazed the paths before us. We, as followers, are allowed options our pioneer brethren did not have. Over 200,000 large and small businesses have moved from Microsoft Office. Big companies like General Electric, Procter & Gamble, Prudential, and L'Oreal have already moved their Web collaboration and branding presence over to Google Apps. On the first day Google Apps was launched, two of the top 25 companies in the world were on board and hosted by Google.

Universities like Northwestern (14,000 students), Arizona State (65,000 students), Trinity College in Dublin, Ireland (15,000 students), and Hofstra University (13,000 students) are a few of the educational institutions using Google Apps every day to manage their business on the Web.

On the personal side, the Standard Edition of Google Apps is perfect for families wanting to stay in touch, as well as church groups, government agencies, communities, groups of friends, and other personal and professional entities that want to work on the Web.

My personal site, Boles University, has been running on Google Apps since the service was available. In the next chapter, and every chapter after that, I will show you how I set up Boles University to use every inch and byte of the service to provide a solid experience, good service, and reliable Web branding. Follow my template and learn from my mistakes, and you will be live in the ether of Google Apps.

As you can see, Google Apps has a rich, if brief, history of successes, and the beautiful part of that is this: You benefit from those who came and conquered before you, and you are using the exact same bandwidth, service, and Google machines as the big boys. That's a tempting offer of excellence you can accept and enjoy throughout this book.

2 Preparing Your Domain

In this chapter, I'll show you how to get set up. I'll help you purchase a new domain, or in the case of BolesUniversity.com, I'll show you how to use an existing domain with Google Apps.

This is an important chapter filled with warnings and caveats, so even if you're a Web hosting pro and you understand about CNAMEs and MX records–I'll dive into that soon if I already confused you a bit–you should not skip this chapter unless you want to mess up your initial setup.

> **Caution**
> If you mess up any part of the initial setup and it goes live on Google's end, you generally have to wait five days for the fix to get started and then fixed on Google's end. That five-day waiting period includes problems with domain setup and even munged email address creations!

Tell Me, Is It Safe?

Before I get into the details of setting up your domain, you should know your domain and setup will be secure on the Google Apps service. Security on the Internet is a big concern, and you deserve to know how Google protects you, your domain, and your proprietary information from prying eyes. Google addresses security concerns on several fronts.

Google has security teams assigned to protect the perimeter, where the bad guys try to penetrate the Google safe areas with cyber attacks. Google uses infrastructure defense to mechanically dissuade Dedicated Denial of Service (DDS) attacks. Applications are routinely tested for attack vulnerabilities.

If a threat gets past those initial defenses, Google defaults into a protect and respond mode where viruses, phishing schemes to steal your personal information, and other efforts are squashed before they reach you.

Server Protection

Google uses a farm system of servers—some call this sort of computing system a *grid*—where your information is replicated across many servers around the world. The breaking up of your private information makes it harder for the bad guys to steal your entire information, and that is the beauty of working online with Google Apps. Your information is stored in *the cloud* between the computer you are using and the international Google server network. If you keep your email on the Web, you are actively avoiding threats to your local machine and your internal network.

Imagine if your local computer were stolen and every single email and other bits of information were lost forever. Using Google Apps and keeping all your work on the Web provide you with more individual security, not less, because your information is scattered across the world, and only Google knows where it resides and how to put it back together for you when you officially log in.

Logical Protection

Google either writes its own software or modifies third-party software to meet the Google standard. That means there's no program a bad guy can buy that he can hack into to find vulnerabilities in the code. Google's code is proprietary and protected, and that means you are, too.

Your Google email is encoded and stored in a format Google invented to give fast performance, and it isn't stored in a database or a regular file system. You can't tamper with something you can't find.

Note

Did you know over two-thirds of the email sent is spam? Because of Google's high number of users in its Gmail base, the Google spam filters are accurate, fast, and incredibly reliable.

If It's Good Enough for Google...

As a Google Apps domain user you are using the same infrastructure and file system that Google users and managers use.

Information and management of the Google servers are managed by Google employees only, and they are required to use SSH—a secure Web protocol—to access the servers and services.

Google employs over 10,000 people, and tens of millions of people like you and me use Google services. All those eyes and fingers working together under the Google umbrella provide a special global mind-think that typically means problems are quickly fixed. A problem with Gmail for a Google manager is a problem that gets fixed for you as well.

Personal Protection

Google Docs and Spreadsheets and Presentations are locked down by default from being shared beyond your domain. You control who sees what, when, and why. I'll discuss security issues when collaborating over the Web with Google Apps in Chapter 9.

You can invoke Gmail to use SSL (Secure Sockets Layer) to provide an encrypted email interface, and when working with most Google Apps you can use the HTTPS secure server interface if you are concerned about having the highest possible level of security for your calendar and chats.

Caution

Be aware that at no time do any Google employees have access to your confidential user data. If you are stuck and need help, Google employees are required to ask you to grant them access to your personal user data. That privacy policy will not change without your express written consent.

Welcome to BolesUniversity.com!

I'm going to tease your eye with a few screenshots of BolesUniversity.com to help you decide on the means and the methods of setting up your own domain. You'll need to make some choices during setup, and the best way to give you a taste of how the features work is with screens.

If you haven't done so already, start thinking about the purpose of your domain. If you plan to purchase a domain or even use one you already own:

* Are you providing information?
* Are you hoping to collaborate with others?
* How many people will be using your domain services?
* Do you plan to sell anything?

Tip

Throughout this book, you will put together your domain modularly. You can skip around chapters and set up and work with only the pieces of Google Apps you want to personalize and share. You can enable the features in every chapter or only one or two. The choice is yours.

Here's a quick look at how I've been able to personalize–Google calls this process *private labeling*–my Boles University domain with Google Apps. My brand, my Boles University logo, is part of that private labeling.

Self-Served Homepage

You can create Web pages on your own server but still have them be a bigger part of your Google Apps setup, and I'll discuss how that works in Chapter 6. You can see my privately hosted page for Boles University in Figure 2.1 and live online at http://bolesuniversity.com/home.html.

Figure 2.1

This Boles University Web page is hosted on my private server, not a Google server. You can mix and match Web pages yourself, using Google only, or using both methods.

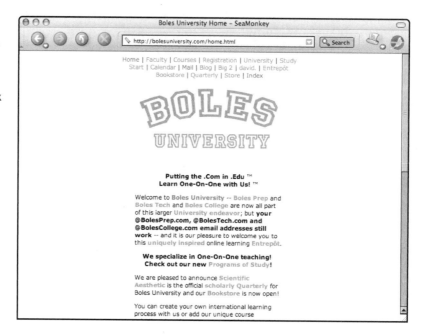

Private Label Start Page

You can brand a start page with your logo for your users. You can pick and choose your content. You can even lock in content so it cannot be changed by your users. Your users can also add widgets and information to their start pages, which I'll show you how to do in Chapter 7. You can view the Boles University start page in Figure 2.2 and live online at http://start.bolesuniversity.com.

Private Label Gmail

The core of Google Apps for you, as the administrator, and for your users is Gmail. You'll learn how to set up and manage all your users in Chapter 4. You can add your logo to brand the Gmail interface, as I have done for Boles University in Figure 2.3. You can visit the branded login page here: http://mail.bolesuniversity.com.

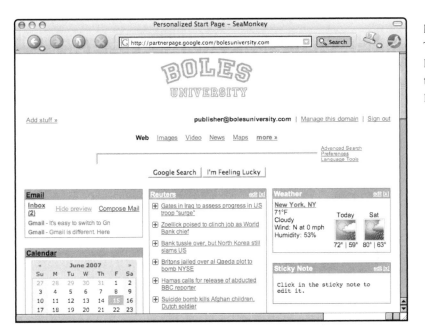

Figure 2.2
This is the start page for Boles University. I was able to brand this page with the Boles University logo.

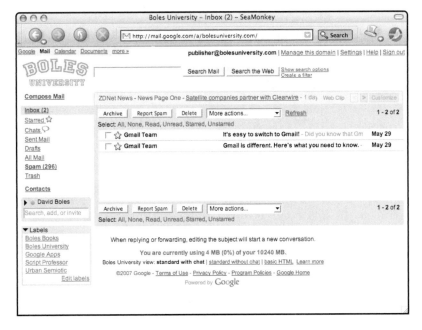

Figure 2.3
This is the branded Boles University Gmail interface for Google Apps.

Private Label Calendar

Google's Calendar App is extremely powerful for sharing information and reserving resources. You will work on getting your calendar working just right across your domain and users in Chapter 5. Figure 2.4 shows the branded Google Calendar for Boles University. The private label login page is located at http://calendar.bolesuniversity.com.

Figure 2.4

This is your domain's private label Calendar view. You can share resources and give others access to your calendar.

Private Label Docs and Spreadsheets

Easy collaboration is a big part of using Google Apps, and when it comes to writing and sharing information, Google Docs and Spreadsheets and Presentations are all part of the tantalizing Google Apps productivity package. You can add other collaborators. You can even share information outside your user domain. The screenshot of the Boles University Docs and Spreadsheets interface found in Figure 2.5 is empty right now. I'll show you how to fill it up with files in Chapter 9. The private label Docs and Spreadsheets URL for Boles University is http://docs.bolesuniversity.com.

Private Label Blog

Blogging is an excellent way to communicate your message to the world and to hold open discussions with friends and new associates. I'll show you how to get a blog working with your domain in Chapter 8. As you can see in Figure 2.6, I have set up Google's Blogger to work with my Boles University domain. You can hit that blog live right now by jamming over to http://blog.bolesuniversity.com.

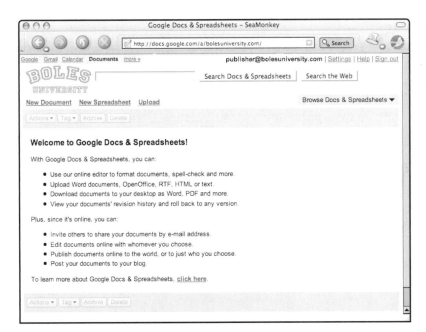

Figure 2.5
This is the main page for working with Google Docs and Spreadsheets and Presentations.

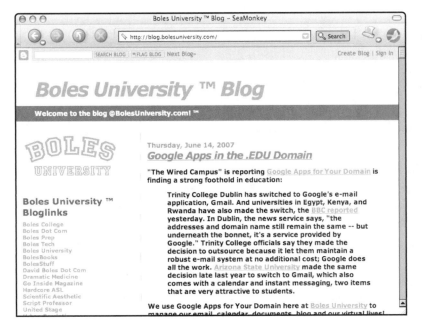

Figure 2.6
This is the Boles University blog, running on Google's Blogger and embedded within the Google Apps service.

Private Label Web Pages

In addition to hosting Web pages on your personal server, you can also let Google host all your Web pages or only some of them by setting up a sub-domain of your domain, such as http://david.bolesuniversity.com, so users can hit you in two places. You will use Google Pages to work that Web site magic, and I'll help you set up your shazam in Chapter 6. I like the split Web page hosting approach because I can run some pages on my server and serve up other Google-specific pages and widgets, as demonstrated in Figure 2.7.

Figure 2.7
This funky and colorful Web page is hosted by Google Apps, and it was created for Boles University using Google Pages.

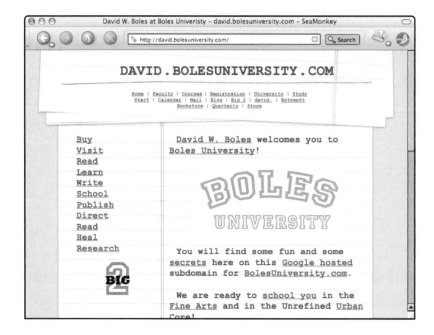

Picking the Right Domain

Before you sign up for Google Apps, make sure you have a good domain name in mind if you don't already own one. As Shakespeare wrote in his great play, *Othello,* "He that filches from me my good name robs me of that which enriches him and makes me poor indeed."

Your domain name is everything. It is your brand and your label. People will type it with their fingers to get their eyes in touch with your content. Your initial sacred covenant is picking a name that sings to you. A .COM domain name is always better than a .NET or .ORG domain, but original .COM names are getting harder and harder to invent. Here are a few things for you to consider:

* Don't dismay if your company name or desired domain is already taken.
* You can always add to the domain name you want by including a number or an "inc" to indicate you are incorporated.
* Pick a domain name that is short and easy to type: DomainInc.COM is better than DomainIncorporated.COM.
* Do a few Google Web searches on the domain name you want before you register to see who else is competing with you in that war of keywords.
* Think categories. If your name describes you, your company, and your niche, then you will have a unique name that will stand the test of domain renewals and Web visitations.

Note

If you purchase your domain from Google Apps, the following top-level domains are currently supported: .COM, .NET, .ORG, .BIZ, and .INFO. If you "bring your own domain" because you've already pre-registered a domain with your own registrar elsewhere, you should be able to use that domain with Google Apps.

Splitting the Baby

Once you've picked your domain name, you need to decide if you want Google to register your domain or if you want to register it yourself. Google uses GoDaddy and eNom to register your domain for you at a cost of $10.00 USD per year.

I prefer to have my domain registrations hosted elsewhere, and I split the baby because I have over 200 domains, and I like everything under one umbrella for easy renewals and management. Network Solutions is my domain registrar and yes, they're monolithic and yes they're expensive, but they've been my partner on the Web since the early 1990s and so we're stuck with each other. I will show you how to set up your domain to work with Google Apps if you decide to go it alone like me.

I also prefer splitting the hosting of my Google Apps service between my private server and Google's setup. This way, if Google goes down, I can make changes on my end to get my site back up, and if my server dies, I can move my Web pages and other vital information right into the Google hosting.

Being on my own means I don't get any automatic Google handholding, and I am wholly responsible for my own MX, CNAME, and DNS zone file entries–and I'll show you how to set all that up using my dedicated virtual server located at Media Temple. If you don't know what any of that means, you should probably have Google set you up.

> **Caution**
> Think carefully if you want Google to set up your domain registration for you, because if you decide you want to change to another domain registrar, you will have to wait 60 days before you can make that change. That's a federally enforced ICANN (Internet Corporation for Assigned Names and Numbers) policy to protect you against scammers and domain thieves–so there's nothing you or Google can do to change the mandatory waiting period.

Tying the Gordian Knot

If you decide to "go all in" and have Google register your domain and host everything, you will get the following benefits to ease your mind:

* Automatic renewal of your yearly $10.00 USD domain registration fee.
* Your personal information will be hidden from public view when people do a WHOIS on you.
* You don't have to set up anything like CNAME, DNS, or MX! Google does it all for you.
* You can control all your DNS settings from your Google Apps Dashboard, and I'll show you that keen Dashboard in Chapter 3.
* Your domain will be locked. That means it belongs to you, and no outsiders can steal it from you.

Signing Up for Service

Now that you have a great .COM name in mind or one that you already own, let's get you set up with the Google Apps service!

Point a Web browser to http://google.com/a and you will see a similar screen as shown in Figure 2.8, where you are presented with an introduction for signing up for service. When you're ready to begin, click on the Get Started button and move on to the next step.

Picking Your Poison

Now it's time for you to decide which flavor of Google Apps you want to run. The Standard Edition is free, and you can have 1,000 or more user accounts. The Premier Edition is more expensive in that each user account will cost you $50.00 USD a year. The Education Edition is available to those institutions that own, operate, and control an .EDU domain.

Figure 2.8
This is the sign-up screen for Google Apps.

Tip

You cannot currently "mix and match" paid and free accounts on Google Apps. Either you pay for all your user accounts or you get them all free. Having the ability to have a few paid accounts and lots of free accounts is an important flexibility that Google will have to address quickly in order to stay competitive in the hosted apps market. Stay tuned!

I am a Premier Edition person all the way for the following reasons:

* You get what you pay for. When you pay your way, you get a private PIN number, and you can call Google directly if you need technical help or if something is broken. Consider that most companies charge you $50.00 USD for one incident, and you are covered for the entire year even if you are the only paid user on your domain.

* I hate advertising! When I pay for my user accounts I can choose to turn off all the Gmail advertising in the sidebar. I won't lose the automatic lookup functionality of street addresses and packages tracking in the sidebar. I'm only losing the everyday ordinary shill.

* I love 10 gigs of email space! I thought 2 gigs was almighty, but 2 is nothing compared to 10. I now have tons of room for all my mail and file attachments and I never have to delete anything ever again. Well...for now, at least!

Okay, I'm clicking on the Sign Up button for the Premier Edition, shown in Figure 2.9.

Figure 2.9
This is your first Google Apps decision: Which flavor of the service do you want to choose?

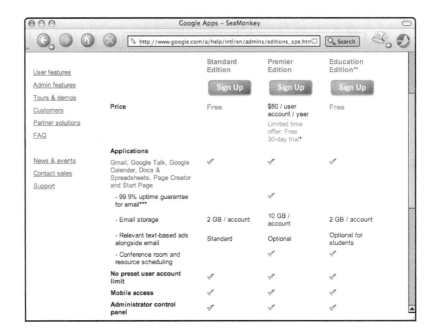

You will need to tell Google whether you have a domain. You will need a Google account to begin the process of signing up. If you have a Google account, you can simply log in. If you need an account, you'll be prompted by Google to sign up for one. Figure 2.10 shows you the first choice you need to make: Do you have a domain or do you need one? I already have one, and I'm ready to go!

Giving Up the Information

Next in the signup process, you need to give Google your domain name. If you picked a different service on the Sign Up page, your screen will look a little different than this one. Provide the information indicated in Figure 2.11, after which point you'll need to pay for and finalize setting up your domain and set up your initial Administrator account.

Thinking About Users

If you have a lot of users you plan to add for any edition of Google Apps, you should be thinking of a good way to bring them all up to speed on the new interface and collaboration methods. If you are transitioning users from one email system to Google Apps, give your users plenty of notice about the change so they can prune their calendars and email inboxes. Google provides this nifty timeline, as seen in Figure 2.12, for setting up a smooth transition over a two-week period.

Figure 2.10
Do you have a domain or do you want Google to register one for you?

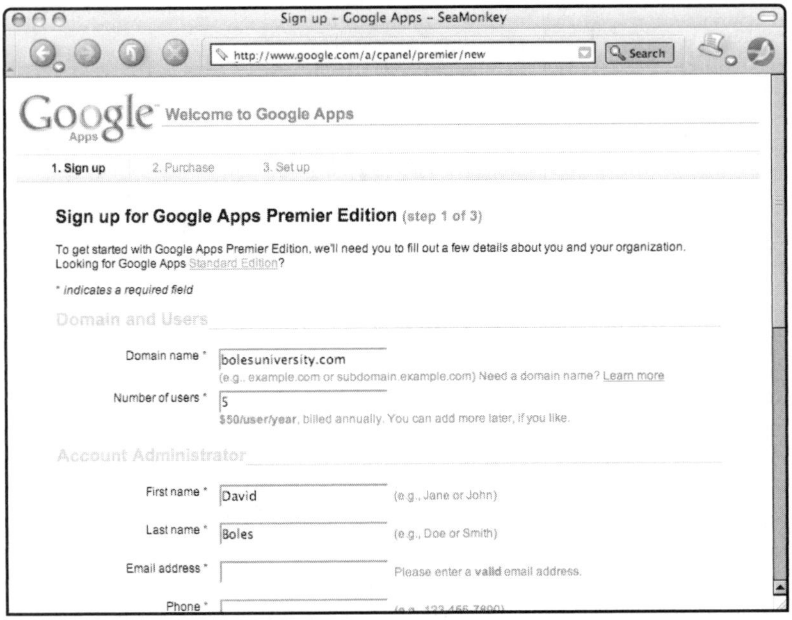

Figure 2.11
This is the Sign Up screen for the Premier Edition of Google Apps.

Figure 2.12
This is the timeline Google
recommends for a smooth
transition for your current
user base.

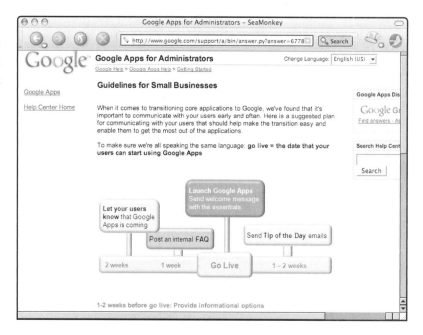

Not So Fast: Measure Twice, Cut Once

Let me remind you one last time that signing up for service with Google Apps takes a lot of
consideration because making the wrong choice could end up costing you money. Remember:
Uncertainty is an expensive bedfellow. Make sure you choose the flavor of Google Apps you
want before you sign up, because it is easier to move up to the Premier Edition from the Standard
Edition than the other way around.

You currently get a 30-day free trial with the Premier Edition. If your credit card is charged after
your free trial period, you're stuck for a year with the Premier Edition. You can't get a refund.
You can't get a prorated rebate if you decide, after six months, to drop down to the free Standard
Edition. In fact, the link to downgrade to the Standard Edition disappears after your 30-day free
trial is over.

Before your first year is up, you can uncheck the box in your account settings so the Premier
Edition no longer auto-renews every year. Then you can downgrade to the Standard Edition
without losing any settings or information. The default setting is to auto-renew every year, so
pay attention to the calendar if you need to make a service change before the year is over.

Caution

The Premier Edition gives you a 10 gig email box, and the Standard Edition is locked into an unchanging and unforgiving 2 gigs. If you want to downgrade before your free trial ends or after your first year is over, you need to make sure your email storage is below the 2 gig limit for the Standard Edition or you will not be allowed to downgrade.

Google will help you set up a main Administrator account. That is a vital process you must accept or you cannot manage your domain. If you move from the Education Edition to the Premier Edition, remember to preserve your Administrator account! Keep everything the same if you move or switch anything because if you get locked out of your own domain you will only have yourself to blame. Google will ask you whether you want to delete your Administrator account. Beware of what you allow to happen!

Signed Up: What Next?

If you signed up with Google to manage your DNS and zone files, you might not need to follow the help provided in this next section. If you are ready to take a domain you already manage and make it work with Google Apps, let's get started right now!

Checking DNS

The first thing you should do is log in to your DNS manager and make certain your entries are pointing in the right direction. DNS means *domain name system*, and it functions as a way to reliably manage and interact with Web sites and Web visitors across the world.

You will have at least two DNS IP entries to make. Some server systems require three or more IP entries to establish your DNS. DNS allows people to use words to find you on the Internet instead of having to type the numbers of an IP address.

In Figure 2.13 I have logged in to my DNS manager: Network Solutions. You can see that my Designated DNS for BolesUniversity.com is pointing to NS1.mediatemple.net and NS2.mediatemple.net. Those are the correct entries for my hosting system on the Media Temple host servers.

Editing Zone Files

Now I have to log in to my Media Temple account so I can manipulate the zone file for BolesUniversity.com. *Zone file* is a fancy term for "telling my server what to do." If I want my domain to be broken into sub-domains and to point to other servers, I can do that by creating a setting in my zone file.

If I want to manage my mail and my Web site, I can make and change entries in my zone file to make sure my Web server effectively communicates those directives to the rest of the world.

Figure 2.13
Check your DNS entries for
your domain to make sure
they are pointing to the
correct hosting server.

Figure 2.14 indicates my WebControl panel for BolesUniversity.com, where I can manage every
aspect of my domain. At the bottom of the page in the DNS zone, I can click on Edit Zone and
be taken to a screen where I can directly manipulate my zone file.

Figure 2.14
Media Temple's
WebControl for
BolesUniversity.com gives
me direct access to my
zone file.

Note

Not all Web hosting services provide zone file access to you as an end user. If you want total control over your Web site, you need to look for a Web host that provides you with the unfettered ability to manipulate your zone file.

Making MX Records

After clicking on Edit Zone, I am taken to the Edit Zone screen at Media Temple, where I can manipulate anything and everything for my BolesUniversity.com setup. Your zone file interface might look different than mine, but you should have the same sort of functionality available if your host provides you this sort of low-level site access.

At the bottom of Figure 2.15 you will see an entry typed into a text box that says "bolesuniversity.com" and a drop-down selection for "MX" and information typed into a data field: "1 aspmx.l.google.com." (that's an "L" not a "one" in the server address).

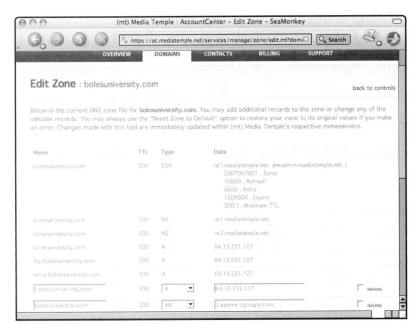

Figure 2.15
In this zone file interface, I can add and delete MX records for BolesUniversity.com so I can get mail working with the Google Apps service.

MX means *Mail Exchange.* MX records point the email you receive and send to the right place. Because I don't want to run email for Boles University on Media Temple, I need to delete all the current MX records and create new multiple entries that are Google Apps-specific.

> **Caution**
>
> Not all MX entries are created equal. You need to know precisely what MX entries your Web host requires. Google keeps an official list of MX entries that are known to work with various hosting companies, and you can find it online here: http://www.google.com/support/a/bin/answer.py? answer=33352.
>
> The biggest mistake most people make when setting up their MX records to work with Google Apps is including the wrong MX records or supplying an incomplete list of MX entries.

MX records are listed in order of priority. The lower the number of the MX record, the greater priority the entry has when interacting with other mail servers. You must set the MX priority when you make your entries. Some Web hosts have a separate zone file entry for the MX priority, whereas others, like Media Temple as seen in Figure 2.16, place the MX priority and address all on the same line.

Don't worry about the CNAME entries and the TXT entry you see for SPF—they're both coming up next in this chapter. We'll set all of those CNAME and SPF entries together later for the specific services you want to install in your Google Apps setup. Consider that a formal tease!

Figure 2.16
Here are all the Google Apps MX entries I had to add to my Boles University zone file to get my email working.

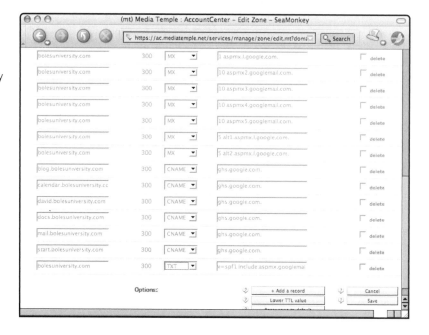

MX Priority and the Trailing Dot

One thing you might immediately notice about MX records is each entry has a priority–Google uses priorities between 1 and 10 for most hosting services–but the thing many people miss is adding the "final dot" in the MX record mail server address. Every MX (and CNAME) entry you will make in your domain setup requires the trailing dot.

Some Web hosts automatically enter the trailing dot for you if you forget to type it in, whereas other servers only take live what you type and save. If you typed the record incorrectly, your mail servers will not work right, and you'll have to figure out on your own how you went wrong.

The "Can't Miss" MX Entries

I am providing you the following MX entries that I am currently using for Boles University because Media Temple is not listed on the official Google site with MX entries that are known to work. These MX entries are the default and perhaps overkill, but they work:

Priority	Mail Server
1	ASPMX.L.GOOGLE.COM.
5	ALT1.ASPMX.L.GOOGLE.COM.
5	ALT2.ASPMX.L.GOOGLE.COM.
10	ASPMX2.GOOGLEMAIL.COM.
10	ASPMX3.GOOGLEMAIL.COM.
10	ASPMX4.GOOGLEMAIL.COM.
10	ASPMX5.GOOGLEMAIL.COM.

Top Priority

If you are unable to add that many entries to your zone file, the most important entry is the first one:

ASPMX.L.GOOGLE.COM.

That's an "L" after "ASPMX" and not the number one; but you should make the MX priority for that entry "1" if you can. You must have at least that entry in your MX record list or your mail will not work with Google Apps. If you are only able to assign one MX record without including a priority number, enter that address. And don't forget the trailing dot!

Touch That!

You will probably need to delete existing MX records in your default zone file mail setup. You cannot have your mail pointing to Google Apps and your server. I had to delete an MX entry for Webmail (webmail.bolesuniversity.com) and for general mail receiving and sending (mail.bolesuniversity.com).

Don't Touch That!

Some Web hosts refuse to let you touch your zone file. Their rationale for that brutal stance is they don't want you messing up everything, requiring someone on their end having to go in and fix it for you. If I mess up my zone files at Media Temple, I can fix the error myself by clicking on a button that will return my zone file to the default setup. Then, I can customize the zone file again to work with Google Apps.

If All Else Fails, Try Begging

Over the last five years, more and more Web hosting companies are allowing end user access to zone files. If you have a hosting company you love or are locked into, but they won't let you into your zone file, here's precisely what Google needs you to say to them in an email to get your MX entries to work with Google Apps:

"I recently signed up for a service called Google Apps. It allows me to use Google applications with my domain name. My domain is hosted with you and I need help in changing the MX records. To use Google for email, I have to point the MX records for my domain to Google's mail servers.

Since Google is not a domain host, they aren't able to configure the MX records for my domain.

There are seven MX records. The first one is ASPMX.L.GOOGLE.COM. and it should have the highest priority. This is the most important MX record.

If I can have more MX records, each should have a lower priority level. The remaining MX records are:

ALT1.ASPMX.L.GOOGLE.COM.

ALT2.ASPMX.L.GOOGLE.COM.

ASPMX2.GOOGLEMAIL.COM.

ASPMX3.GOOGLEMAIL.COM.

ASPMX4.GOOGLEMAIL.COM.

ASPMX5.GOOGLEMAIL.COM.

Once these MX records are configured correctly, I'll be able to receive mail for my domain in my Google Apps email accounts."

So there! Google did your niggling for you, and you shouldn't have to worry whether the instructions to your domain host are clear, because Google certainly knows the terminology and language to use to communicate with similar techies.

The CNAME Tease

Okay, I teased you a moment ago about CNAME entries. By the time you're done with this book and you have all your Google Apps services up and running, you're going to be sick of CNAMES! Here's a bit of what's to come.

CNAME is short for *Canonical Name,* and you enter a CNAME into the zone file for your domain to create an alias for the real name of your server. An example of this is "mail.bolesuniversity.com" where the "mail" part of that Web address is the CNAME.

I'm mentioning this now because you might need to add a CNAME entry in order for Google to verify your domain, and it will be something obnoxious like "googlefffgggghhh34435665." You can delete that atrocity after Google lets you know you domain is verified. If you don't have direct access to your zone file, it's time to fire up another Google email template and make that direct request to your Web host.

Note

CNAMES are also called *third-level domains* or *sub-domains,* and you can think of a Web site address as a series of hierarchies. The top-level domain is what appears after the "dot" or period in the Web site name. In the BolesUniversity.com Web site address, the .com is the top level. The second-level domain for BolesUniversity.com is BolesUniversity and the CNAME. The third-level domain is added to the front of that address to create a sub-domain like "mail.BolesUniversity.com," where "mail." creates the third-level domain.

Begging a Second Time

Here's what Google recommends you say to your Web host via email to create a CNAME on your behalf:

"I recently signed up for a service called Google Apps. It allows me to use Google applications with my domain name. My domain is hosted with you, and I need help in creating a CNAME record. To verify that I own my domain name, I want to create a special CNAME record. Since Google is not a domain host, they aren't able to create the CNAME record.

The information I have from Google is a unique string for the CNAME record and a destination.

The string is [look in the Control Panel. It will look similar to googlefffgggghhh34435665].

The destination is google.com.

Basically, there should be a CNAME record for [insert string].my_domain.com that points to google.com. [Remember to replace my_domain.com with your actual domain name.]

Once the CNAME record is created correctly, I'll be able to use several of the Google applications for my domain."

SPF Records: Not Just Suntan Protection Anymore

One great thing Google added to their mail setup is a pretty little thing called *Sender Policy Framework*, or SPF for short. You want this. You need SPF protection for your mail because SPF lets you tell the world which mail hosts you approve for sending your mail.

That's important and protective because having a SPF installed in your zone file means you will be better able to defend against those awful spammers who forge the "From:" address with your email address and make life really miserable for you as innocent, yet angry, end users seek you out to tell you off for sending them spam when you never did.

Google really wants you to set up a TXT (text) entry in your DNS zone file, but the ugly part is not all Web hosts or domain registrars allow you to easily enter a TXT record right now.

It fascinates me that Network Solutions does not allow TXT zone file entries, but Media Temple does allow TXT records. If you can add a TXT record for your domain, here's the text you need to include to enable SPF for your domain:

```
v=spf1 include:aspmx.googlemail.com ~all
```

Lowering TTL

When you're finished setting up your zone file, lower the TTL value–the Time-to-Live value–if you can because that means your zone file will be updated more quickly in the IP (Internet Protocol) packet sent to your network router. The TTL value refreshes the network–sort of like a mouthwash rinse–where the old zone file information is "spit out" and replaced by your new information. A lower TTL will make your changes "live" on the Web faster as it propagates throughout the Internet.

> **Caution**
>
> Not all domain hosts allow you to lower your TTL. That means you might be stuck with their default setting that could range anywhere form five minutes to five days, depending on their setup. That's another reason why you should choose your domain host prudently and wisely, because sometimes it's worth paying more for greater control over your domain.

The Virtue of Patience

You've done a fine job so far! Now you get to take a break and wait a little bit. It takes time for your zone fine DNS changes, CNAME additions, MX records, TTL changes, and SPF records to update across routers all over the world. This process used to take around three days a few years ago, and during that time your Web site would appear and disappear and then finally appear for good after a few days.

Today, things are much faster. Zone file changes happen almost immediately on an established domain. If you have a new name, you might have a wait a few hours or even a day or two for everything to propagate and update. Don't panic. Don't sweat if one minute you can hit your mail server and then find it unavailable the next hour. That's the nature of the Web. It's more wait than hurry up.

WHOIS Confirmation

After you've waited a day or so for your zone file changes to take effect, you should fire up your favorite WHOIS authority and check to see whether your changes have propagated across the Internet. My favorite WHOIS client is a free online service called CentralOps.net (http://centralops.net). By clicking on the Domain Dossier link, you can then type in the name of your domain and get one of the fastest and most fulfilling returns of information available on the Web.

In Figure 2.17 you can see the WHOIS results for BolesUniversity.com. All my MX entries appear to have propagated, including my SPF text record!

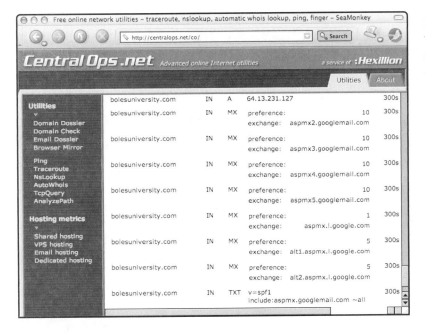

Figure 2.17

The WHOIS client at CentralOps.net confirms the MX records for BolesUniversity.com have propagated across the Internet.

If you want to monitor your domain on a deep level to make sure everything goes well between your setup and Google's, you might be interested in using a service like DNS Stuff, located at http://dnsstuff.com, where you can get hardcore feedback on what's up with your domain. In Figure 2.18, DNS Stuff confirms that my DNS service for BolesUniversity.com is correctly pointing to Media Temple, and I am told in plain English what all these settings mean.

Figure 2.18
DNS Stuff provides low-level reports on how your DNS service is set up in easy-to-read English.

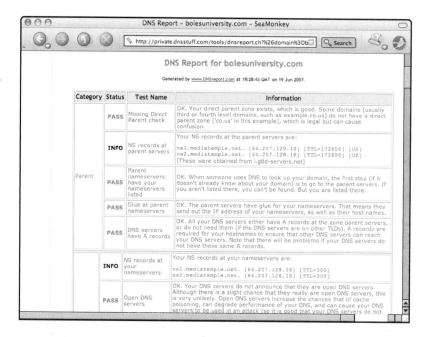

If I scroll down the page a bit on my DNS Stuff report for BolesUniversity.com as demonstrated in Figure 2.19, I get a big red failure for having "duplicate MX records" on my domain.

Figure 2.19
DNS Stuff gives my MX Google-specific records a failing grade!

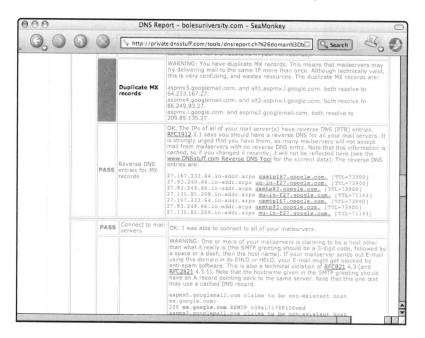

It appears that Google has two Web addresses using the same IP address, and although that isn't a great thing, Google is famous for not revealing the MX IP addresses to push spammers away from their servers.

Round Robin Mail Servers

Instead of using single dedicated IP addresses for mail servers like everyone else on the Web does, Google instead chooses to use generic name addresses, and they then cleverly rotate IP addresses associated with those name servers to confuse and confound the spammers.

That's good for us, but that method of "round robin mail server protection" sort of breaks things like reports from DNS Stuff and other ISPs because they cannot pin down Google's mail servers in order to white-list them as safe and verified.

Google will not provide static IP addresses, and so sometimes Google's name servers get blacklisted, and mail doesn't get delivered. If you find you cannot send mail, or if you get complaints that your email isn't getting received, be sure to get in touch with Google to let them know of your trouble.

Trust, But Verify

Once you have verified your zone file changes are active through a WHOIS search like dnsstuff.com that is not provided by your domain host, you need to prove to Google that you are who you claim you are: the domain owner.

Google needs you to prove ownership because there are a lot of unkind and scummy people on the Web who might want to set up Google Apps using your domain even though they don't own your domain!

For big domains with lots of users and administrators, Google also needs you to confirm that you specifically have the appropriate backend access to control the domain before they make Google Apps active on their end.

Tip

If you purchased your domain through Google when you first signed up, then you're cool. Google already knows you and the domain control power you have.

Google Says What?

Google has two methods in place that will help you prove you claim to your domain: You can upload an HTML file to your Web server via FTP or you can create a special CNAME entry in your DNS zone file.

I remind that you Google makes you jump through these verification hoops for your own good to provide security, privacy, and a bit of a challenge to make sure you're cut out to have Google Apps hosting setup split between your server and the Google Apps service.

In your Google Apps welcome letter, you will be instructed how to log in to your Control Panel to begin the verification process.

Note

You will not be able to activate your Google Apps until you verify your domain. You have 30 days to complete the verification process or Google will delete your domain because they will assume you are not the rightful owner of the domain name.

The Return of the Dreaded CNAME

The first choice, and the silliest, as discussed earlier in this chapter, is to create a wacky CNAME entry consisting of a special string of characters such as "googlefffgggghhh34435665. bolesuniversity.com" and then point it to google.com. Be aware that the silly string of letters and numbers is different for every domain, so make sure you write it down for your verification!

Sometimes just having your MX records in place and propagated is enough to get verified via the CNAME Google verification test.

Remember that adding a CNAME can take around 48 hours to propagate, so this isn't a quick way to verify your domain. You might want to try the HTML file form of verification for a faster start.

Tip

If you do create the silly CNAME entry, make sure you go back later and delete the entry from your zone file after Google verifies you. There's no need to clutter up your zone file with meaningless cruft!

HTML File

If you have some Web site creation experience and FTP access to your domain, the HTML file upload is the best way to verify your domain for Google. Here are the steps you need to take to get there:

1. Make sure you have a unique string from Google to verify your domain—it should look something like "googlefffgggghhh34435665."
2. Make an HTML file and paste that unique string into the body of your file.

3. Name your HTML file googlehostedservice.html.

4. Upload the file to your Web server via FTP and place it in the home directory.

5. Visit your Web site and type in the full name of the file—something like http://bolesuniversity.com/googlehostedservice.html—to make sure the file is there and readable.

6. Visit your Google Control Panel and use the HTML choice to verify your domain. You should be verified in seconds, or certainly within 48 hours!

Caution

Usually HTML verification is instantaneous. You tell Google to look for the HTML file, it does, and you're good and done. However, if you have to wait longer than 48 hours for HTML verification, be sure to check your HTTP server logs for any attempts by Google to verify you.

If you see a 412 error code—that a precondition failed—related to your googlehostedservice.html file, that means the verification process is getting trapped in your Apache mod_security condition.

You can fix this on your own by creating or adding to your .htaccess file in your root directory the following line:

```
SecFilterEngine Off
```

Save your .htaccess file, and Google verification should continue normally.

If You Need Help

Sometimes getting help with Google Apps can be a problem if you aren't using the Premier or Education Edition. You can find help online in the Google Apps Help Center:

http://www.google.com/support/a

You will fill out a contact form and hope to hear back from someone sometime.

PIN

If you are using the Education or Premier Edition, you will have a PIN number and a toll-free telephone number you can call to request help. I have used the service, and it's worth every cent.

Google claims they provide 24/7 phone support, but I find it's more like 18/5 because after business hours and on the weekends you won't talk to a live person. You'll instead be invited to leave voice mail and a hope for a callback the next business day.

Google Groups

One of the quickest ways to get help online from others users, as well as from the new Google Groups Advisors, is to head over to Google Groups at http://groups.google.com and search for the Google Apps Discussion Group, as indicated in Figure 2.20.

Figure 2.20
Google Groups can provide fast answers to problems that frustrate you.

Once you're in the Google Apps Discussion Group, you can search for help on a topic that frustrates you, or you can post a new message for help. Sometimes you'll get an answer right away, and other times it can take days for a resolution. Figure 2.21 is the Google Groups home-page for Google Apps; you can see there's lots of action and discussion going on all day every day.

Figure 2.21
This is the end user support homepage for Google Apps on Google Groups.

WARNING!: Spammers, Scammers, and Phishing

As much as we wish the rest of the world lived as we do–in an honest, upright, moral, and correct manner–we must always be on the watch for those who want to do us harm. Unfortunately, there are people in the world who want your domain and who will seek to corrupt your endeavors.

There's always the danger of scaring people, but we now live in a world where lots of rogues with bad intent are looking to hurt you for fun or do some monetary damage to your good name by ripping off your good will.

Tip

Phishing is a criminal act intended to steal your personal information by tricking you into thinking you are dealing with a trusted entity. Phishing is extremely successful because it relies on your kind heart and good intentions. Phishers typically use email or Instant Messaging to con personal information out of their victims, but sometimes they use online groups to find victims.

As you read in this chapter, verifying your Google Apps domain can be an ongoing and frustrating process. Recently, in the official Google Apps Group, an unsavory entity called

GoogleVerify.com posted hundreds of messages to try to trick users into submitting their Google Apps usernames and passwords.

You can see the fake Web site in Figure 2.22. Even though the site looks sort of official, there is a YouTube video there, and the English is not standard and reads unlike anything you typically will read from Google.

GoogleVerify.com resolves to GVerify.com—so these people are professionals who obviously received a "cease and desist" letter from Google for using the Google name in the name of their domain, so GoogleVerify.com now gets forwarded to GVerify.com. Tricky. Sneaky. Smart. Don't be fooled!

Figure 2.22

GoogleVerify.com and GVerify.com are phishing Web sites created to steal your domain by tricking you into submitting your Google Apps username and password.

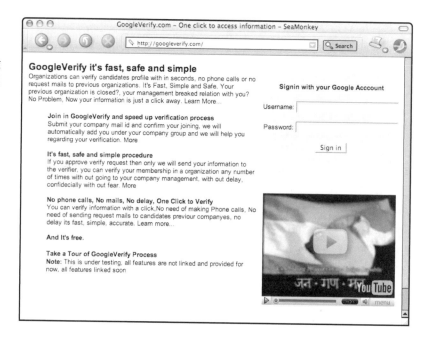

The general Google Apps community leapt on those phishing messages from GoogleVerify.com/GVerify.com and told people the site was a scam, but one always wonders how much damage was done to people hoping to get a quick resolution to their Google Apps verification problems.

One way you can try to verify the veracity of a Web site is to do a CentralOps.net search on the domain name. In Figure 2.23, you can see the WHOIS return GoogleVerify.com. Note that the domain name is not hosted by Google and that google.com is not listed anywhere as a name server in the DNS record.

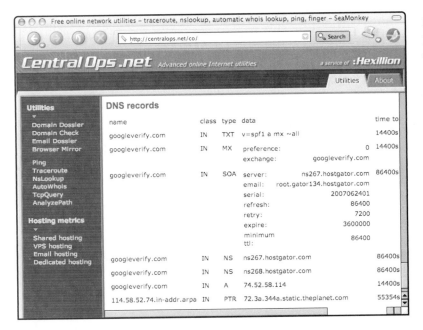

Figure 2.23
Here is the WHOIS report for GoogleVerify.com, proving that the domain, and its desire for your login information, is questionable and not operated by Google.com.

Please be on the lookout for this kind of scam as you tend your domain on the Web. You own something others covet: a good domain name. Don't let them steal that from you or gain access to your private account information.

You're Now a Googleteer, Too!

After completing this chapter you should be all signed up, MX ready, CNAME-d to death, and fully SPF protected, and wholly Google verified! In the next chapter, I'll get into the necessary nitty-gritty of managing your domain online with the Google Apps Dashboard interface.

3   Managing Your Domain

In this chapter, you will log in to your Control Panel and work with your Dashboard view. You will step through the Dashboard setup by filling in the necessary account information and then editing the general settings. Finally, you'll set up some domain aliases so you can immediately expand the power and influence of your single domain.

The chapter is especially image heavy–semiotically tantalizing, if you will–because I believe in the power of navigating and learning through pictures rather than through text. Google has a tendency to change little things here and there, and some steps become one step or three steps. When you try to explain some processes using text and a nugget or two changes, you're forever lost.

By sharing the images of my setup process with you, I ensure that you can find your way back even when the process changes a bit, due to the visual anchors in the Google interface you see and learn about here.

Trolling Your Control Panel

Let's start at the beginning. Log in to your administrator email account and click on the Manage This Domain link found in the upper-right corner of your Google Apps Gmail interface, as indicated in Figure 3.1. This link works best, for me anyway, because I live in Gmail all day long, and I can zoom right in my Google Apps Control Panel with one click.

Now you have to formally log in to manage your Google Apps account. Google provides this extra step of protection to guarantee that you have Administrator privileges to manage the domain.

Enter your username and password and click the Sign In button so you can begin to manage, customize, and review the Control Panel of your domain, as seen in Figure 3.2.

Figure 3.1

You can manage your Google Apps domain by using the link found in the upper-right corner of your Google Apps Gmail interface.

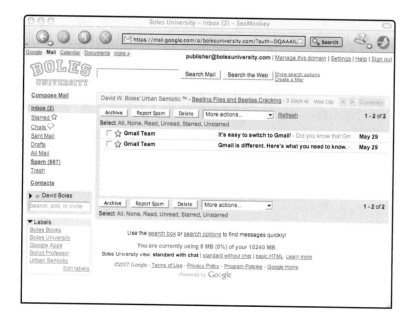

Your login URL looks like this; be sure to replace "bolesuniversity.com" with the domain name you're using: https://www.google.com/a/bolesuniversity.com

Figure 3.2

This is the login interface for Control Panel access to Google Apps.

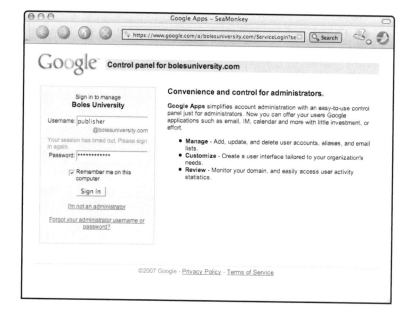

> **Tip**
> The Manage This Domain link found in the upper-right corner of your Google Apps Gmail interface also appears on your customized Google Apps Start Page interface, but interestingly enough, you can't get to your Control Panel from your Google Apps Calendar page or your Google Apps Docs, Spreadsheets, and Presentations main interface page—although you can if you are in the document file upload area.

Driving Your Dashboard

Now you have access to drive your Dashboard. The Dashboard is the brainstem of your Google Apps Control Panel interface, as you can see in Figure 3.3.

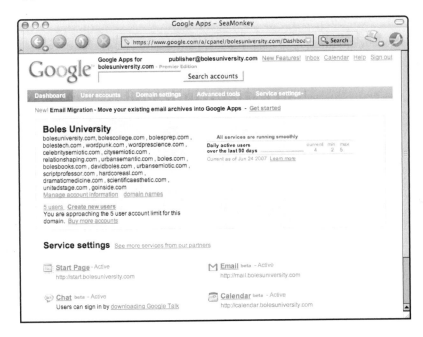

Figure 3.3
This is the Dashboard, your Google Apps brainstem for controlling your domain.

There is a ton of information here to swallow, and we aren't going to drink it all in this chapter. Pay no attention to Service Settings, which includes the Start Page and Email—you'll get to those in Chapters 4 and 7.

Instead, let your eye wander around the middle of Boles University and over to the area in the middle right that says "All services are running smoothly." That's your update screen, and in my experience, it is usually wrong when reporting the status of daily active users over the last 90 days. That graph is currently wrong. I have five active users who are all online right now even though that graph is reporting four. Remember, Google Apps are ever changing and not always perfect, so don't freak out if you see something listed incorrectly.

Now check out the left side of the screen. You see all those domain names listed under the bold head, Boles University? Those are domain aliases, and you're going to set them up in a minute. Notice that the last two domains listed are unitedstage.com and goinside.com, because by the end of the chapter that's going to change. You'll be adding two more domain aliases.

Click on the Manage Account Information link found under those last two domain aliases to head into the next screen, where you'll set some parameters for your domain administration.

The Legend of the Graphic Email

The graphical email function of Google Apps can be confusing because sometimes the information is accurate and other times it is outdated. Here's a quick refresher via a Google Apps Support Legend to help you remember what those terms on the graph really mean in the real world of Google Apps.

"Active Users in the Last 90 Days" means how many email accounts you have "in use" at your domain. Now that seems to mean different things at different times. Sometimes it seems to mean how many email accounts you purchased if you're on the Premier Edition or Education Edition. Sometimes it seems to mean how many people are actually using their email accounts at the time you look at the screen. Other times still, it seems to mean how many users have access their Google Apps Gmail in the last 90 days. How's that for semiclarity?

"Current" means, it seems, how many users are live online at the moment, but because the graph isn't updated live, that number is often wrong or behind or ahead, depending on the involvement of your users.

"Min" means the lowest number of daily active users over the past 90 days. Two appears to be correct for Boles University.

"Max" means the highest number of daily active users in the last 90 days. Five is the correct number for the maximum number of users we have at Boles University right now.

"Current as of Month Day Year" is the date your graph was generated, and notice there is only a date stamp. No timestamp is provided.

The graph is a neat feature, and I'm sure it will be enhanced and expanded to provide even more real-time data, perhaps even after you've purchased this book!

Domain Settings

By clicking on the Manage Account Information link, you are taken into the Domain Settings section of your Google Apps Dashboard. From this area, you can set the intimate nature of how you want your domain to interact with the Internet via Google Apps.

Account Information

The top half of your account information screen provides subscription status and a link for you to purchase more user accounts. You can also choose to have your Google Apps subscription auto-renew each year, as seen in Figure 3.4.

If you have the Premier or Educational Edition, this is where you find your Customer PIN and your Support PIN. I blurred out those numbers because they are linked specifically to Boles University. Don't dial the 800 or 650 numbers to try to charm your way into getting help because you have to enter your PIN information first to get by the robot sentry that answers when you call.

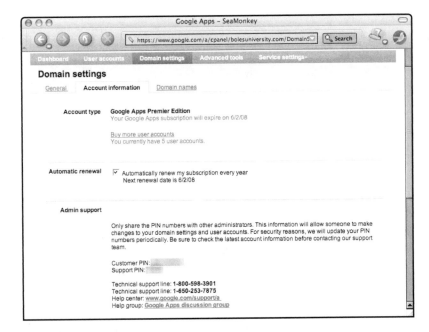

Figure 3.4

This is the top half of your Google Apps account information screen.

> **Note**
> You can pick up the phone and get help directly from Google with those PIN and phone numbers, and in my experience, Google folk are friendly, but they are not on duty to speak to you live 24/7. They are available 18 hours a day five days a week, and you will be asked to leave a voice mail message after hours and during the weekend. You can always try to get off-hours assistance online from the Google Help Center or the Google Apps Help Group.

The bottom half of your account information screen is shown in Figure 3.5, and I have once again blurred the information specific to my account. Your contact information is vitally important because if you have a problem with your Google Apps setup or if Google needs to contact you, that information will be used.

Figure 3.5
Here's the bottom half of your Google Apps account information screen.

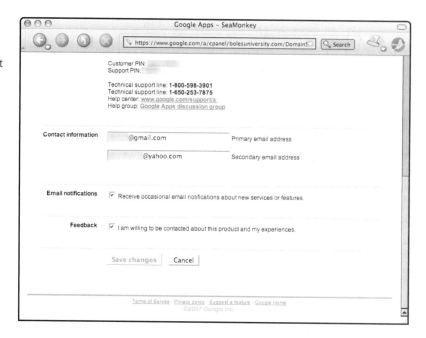

> **Caution**
>
> Do not use any Google Apps email accounts as your contact information. If you have a password problem or if you get locked out or if your entire Google Apps site is unusable, Google will have no way to contact you because your email is hooked into the very domain that isn't working for you!

I like providing feedback to Google. They often providing interesting surveys that I can use to help them improve their services. Make sure that option is checked if you want to help define future feature sets.

I especially like getting email notifications from Google, and as I am writing this, I just received one! You won't get those updates unless you check that box and save that page. You can see their update in Figure 3.6, where they announce a slew of new enhancements gleaned from their feedback surveys!

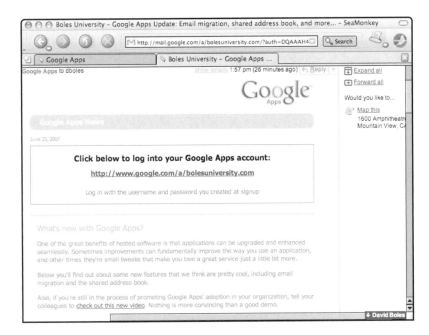

Figure 3.6
Here's an email update from Google provided for their Google Apps subscribers.

General Settings (Logos and More)

Now scroll up to the top of the Domain Settings page and click on the General link to view the top half of the screen, where you can set specific contact information for your domain, as demonstrated in Figure 3.7. You can enter your organization's name and also provide direct contact information. You also set the preferred language for your domain here as well as your default time zone. You can lock in a single time zone, or you can allow your end users to choose their own.

Figure 3.8 indicates the bottom half of your General Domain Settings page, which has lots of interesting stuff you can modify to give your domain a branded, private-label look and feel.

The first thing you'll want to create, if you don't already have one, is a header logo. Header logos will put your logo–your private label brand–on all the Google Apps services that all your users and customers can see. You can accept the default Google Gmail logo and Google Calendar logos if you wish, but why would you?

Fire up your favorite graphics program and create a logo 143 pixels wide and 59 pixels high and save it as a .PNG file. If you don't provide the right size, Google will arbitrarily crop and resize the image, and it probably won't look good. You can also use the .GIF file format, but I find the .PNG format works much better when Google dynamically resizes your logo to fit their pages.

Figure 3.7
This is the top half of your Domain Settings General page.

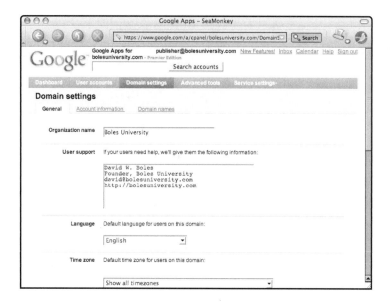

Figure 3.8
Here is the bottom half of your Domain Settings General screen.

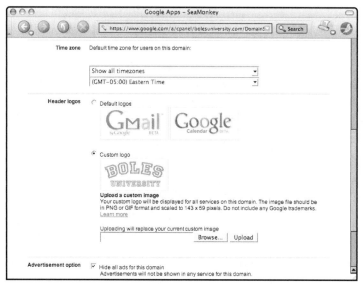

Once you upload you custom logo and click the radio button to make it the active selection, you will see your handcrafted brand on all Google Apps services.

Tip

To have your logo look its best across all browsers and operating systems, be sure to use *Web-safe* colors when you create your logo. Your color palette will be limited, but you will be able to predict how your brand is being viewed across all viewing platforms. Here's a great Google directory site that will give you everything you need to know and learn about making sure your palette is Web safe: http://www.google.com/Top/Computers/Graphics/Web/Colors/.

The last thing you should absolutely enable–if the option appears for the Google Apps edition you selected–is the Hide All Ads for This Domain option. I confess that not having advertising in any Google Apps service is a great thrill. I don't want to be bothered with sales ads while I'm working.

Some people, usually in management positions above you, who are not familiar with how spam and email technology works tend to feel Google is "reading their mail" when those ads are served in Gmail, and they feel their privacy is invaded. It's funny they don't feel that spam-prevention software is "reading their mail," but they feel Google is reading their mail by serving up contextual advertising. You can alleviate any decision-maker concerns about those ads by simply removing them from the purview of your Google Apps service.

Note

If you choose to turn off the advertising for your domain, you will not lose the keen Maps and Package Tracking information that appears in your sidebar while you're reading your Google Apps Gmail. So lose the ads and keep the functionality!

Google Logo and Landing Page Policies

Okay, so you're going to create your own logo. There are a few rules you need to keep in mind while creating that brand or Google might turn off your ability to rebrand their service.

First, you can use the phrase "Powered by Google" anywhere in your logo and on your pages. Sometimes that phrase is just put there permanently by Google, and you can't remove it even if you want to delete it.

You can't touch the Google trademarks. That means you cannot use the words "Google" or "Gmail" or "Google Talk" and the like in your logo.

You are also not allowed to use the Google logo or the Gmail logo or any other Google logo as part of your branded logo.

Finally, you have to own the logo you create. You can't borrow it from another site. That's stealing. Create your own original logo, and then you own it, and you can use it as you wish.

Domain Names

Now it's time to add some more value and depth to your current domain by adding other domains. If you've been around the Web domain business for a while, I'm sure you have a secret stash of fantastic domain names, and you might not yet be using them all. Your Google Apps hosted setup is the perfect way to get Google Apps Gmail working with all those domains under the umbrella of a single primary domain. You don't have to make Web pages for these domain aliases to work. You need only to add them to your Google Apps service and then change the MX records to point to the Google Apps servers, as you did in Chapter 2.

If you don't have any other domains, go get some right now, but register them with a standalone registration service like Network Solutions, because then you can DBA (do business as) a myriad of other entities and brands via email, all at the same time. I'll show you how.

> **Note**
> A domain alias is a keen thing that lets you point one domain at another. You could have http://
> bolesuniversity.net and http://bolesuniversity.org both point to http://bolesuniversity.com, and
> using your registrar's settings, you could have the .NET and .ORG addresses stay that way or "mask"
> themselves and resolve to the .COM address. As a blunt example of this, if you go to http://
> bolescollege.com or http://bolesprep.com or http://bolestech.com, they all become http://
> bolesuniversity.com through domain aliasing and URL masking.

In your Domain Settings Dashboard view, click on Domain Names. As demonstrated in Figure 3.9, you should at least see your primary domain listed in the top half of the screen. You can also see some of the list of domain aliases I have associated with my primary domain.

Most of those domains redirect to other Web sites I own, but until Google Apps, I had no way to get mail at those domains. By setting up those domain aliases, I can now get mail at those domains right in my primary domain Google Apps Gmail inbox. (In Chapter 4, I'll show you how to reply from these domain aliases you set up in this chapter.)

> **Note**
> Even if your email is hosted elsewhere for your domain aliases, you can still get the value and the
> outstanding spam protection of Google Apps Gmail with this system of "One Inbox, Many Domains"
> that I employ. I have 10 gigs of email storage to fill up!

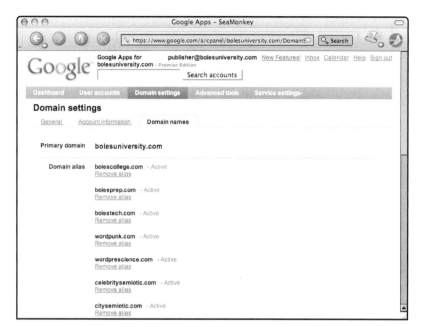

Figure 3.9
This is the top half of my
Domain Names page,
where I can set up my
domain aliases.

Adding a Domain Alias

In Figure 3.10, you see the bottom half of my Domain Names page. There are additional domain aliases of mine that you can see, but I want you to specifically look at the bottom of the page and click on the Add a Domain Alias link to associate another domain with an account. An active domain means the domain is working and is verified by Google as a validly owned and operated domain by you.

> **Tip**
> The general idea is to associate "related" domain aliases such as bolescollege.com and bolesprep.com with the main bolesuniversity.com domain, but I argue you can, and should, go wider and longer than that. For example, I use the domain alias urbansemiotic.com to get email for my Urban Semiotic blog hosted by WordPress.com. Without this Google Apps domain aliasing, and without WordPress.com support for Google Apps, I would have no other way to get email at the UrbanSemiotic.com domain.

Now you need to enter the domain you want to alias, as indicated in Figure 3.10. Make sure you already own the domain, or you will mess up this slick process of domain association.

Figure 3.10
This is the bottom half of the Domain Names page, where you can associate another domain alias with your primary domain.

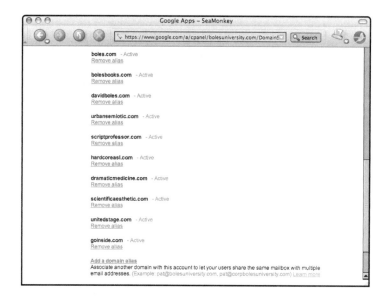

I registered the GAYDbook.com, a Google Apps for Your Domain Book Dot Com domain, so you can send me email! I'll know if you use the david@gaydbook.com email address to get in touch with me that you bought this book and you have a question or a kiss for me. (By the way, I registered that name long before Google shortened the title of their service to Google Apps.)

Click on the Continue and Set Up Email Delivery button to go to the next step.

Figure 3.11
Enter your domain alias to associate it with your primary Google Apps domain.

Setting Up Email Delivery

Now you're back into the realm of the familiar MX records setting you frequented in Chapter 2. This time around I'm not going into Media Temple, my domain host, because my GAYDbook.com domain is being managed at Network Solutions.

Note

If you go to http://GAYDbook.com, you will be redirected to another page for this book (http://bolesbooks.com/thomson), and the domain will be masked so you will only see the GAYDbook.com address in your browser address window.

In Figure 3.12, you can see I selected Network Solutions as the service where I will change my MX records. Google has prepared specific instructions for many domain hosts to help you know how many MX entries you need to make to get your domain alias DNS working.

Heed the warning on that page that changing your MX records might mean messing up your email. If you have existing MX records in your DNS zone file, you need to delete them first and then add the Google Apps–specific MX records to your zone file.

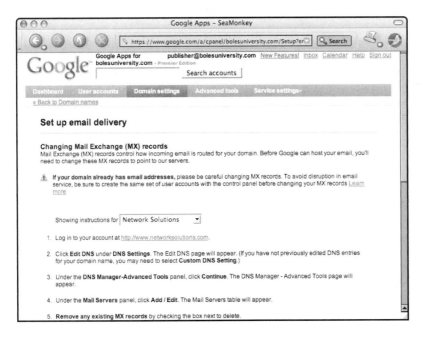

Figure 3.12
I chose Network Solutions as my domain alias DNS host.

In Figure 3.13, you can see I am logged in to my Network Solutions account. I will choose to edit a custom DNS setting.

You can also see at the bottom of that figure that I already have GAYDbook.com pointing, via Web forwarding, to my Boles Books Web page for this book.

Figure 3.13

On this page I need to edit my custom DNS setting for my GAYDbook.com domain.

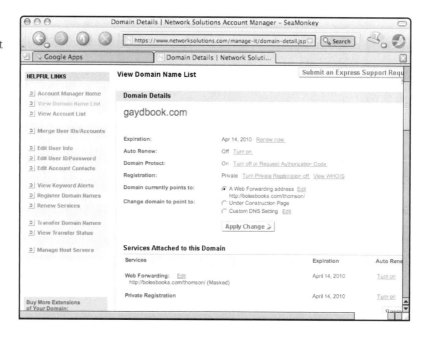

You should get a big fat warning page like the one Network Solutions throws in my face in Figure 3.14. I don't want to move my DNS to another server. I want to use the DNS Manager–Advanced Tools to enter my MX records. Click on the second Continue button to get to that customization page.

Figure 3.15 demonstrates the Advanced Tools interface for GAYDbook.com, and this is where a lot of people get lost in the flush and luster of managing their DNS. I don't want to change my IP address. I don't want to add any CNAME records via my host alias. I only want to add MX records, and so I will click on the Add/Edit button to modify my mail servers.

You can see in Figure 3.16 how different entering MX records is here with Network Solutions than it was with Media Temple in Chapter 2. As well, your domain host might look completely different than what you see here, but I purposefully want to expose you to a variety of domain management interfaces so you can see the similarities.

I have no mail servers set up for GAYDbook.com, so I don't need to delete any existing records. I can just enter the Google Apps MX records and be done with it.

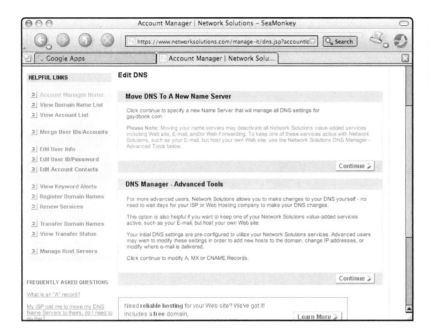

Figure 3.14
This is where I access the advanced setting for my DNS Manager zone file.

Figure 3.15
You modify MX records by choosing to change your mail servers.

Figure 3.16
This is where you enter MX records for a Network Solutions hosted domain name.

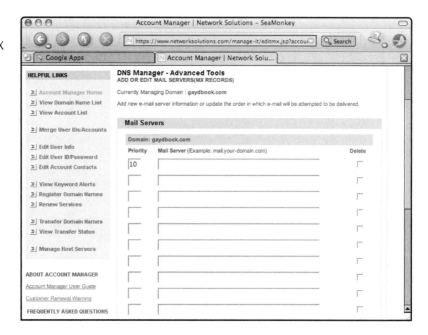

I have to bounce back over to my Google Apps Dashboard so I can copy and paste the recommended MX records from Google over to Network Solutions. This can be a tedious process, and it's easy to mess up if you don't insert the Google mail server names correctly. Make sure you include that trailing period, as seen in Figure 3.17, if you choose to copy and paste the information instead of printing it out and retyping it.

When I'm finished setting up the MX servers, I will come back to this page and click on the I've Completed These Steps button found at the bottom of the Google Apps domain alias setup page.

I bounce between Network Solutions and my Google Apps Dashboard five times to enter all those MX record addresses and their appropriate priority numbers. You can see the end result in Figure 3.18. I click on the Save button to record the new mail server entries.

Tip
Remember when we talked about the importance of adding SPF records to your DNS zone file in Chapter 2 because they help prevent spam? Well... Media Temple provides SPF entries via a TXT entry, but Network Solutions does not! That's a sad fact that I hope remains temporary because Network Solutions needs to find a way to support TXT entries in the Advanced Tools for their DNS Manager so we can protect our email servers with appropriately approved SPF records.

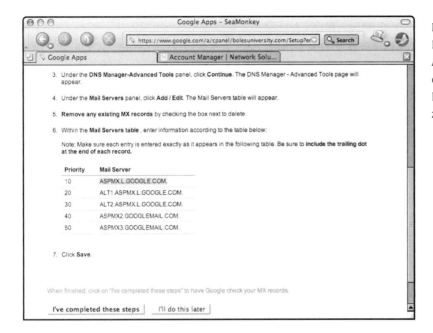

Figure 3.17
I highlighted the Google Apps mail server so I can copy the address into my Network Solutions DNS zone file.

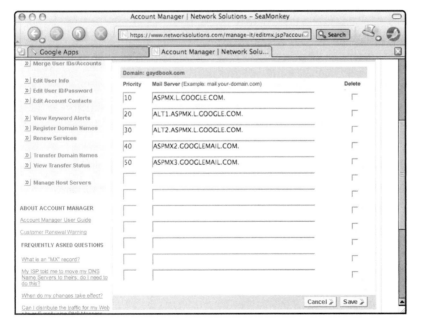

Figure 3.18
I copy and pasted all the MX records into my GAYDbook.com DNS zone file.

You're almost done! Figure 3.19 indicates the status of my saved MX records. I have to confirm the changes for them to take effect and be propagated and updated across the Internet. I click on Continue to activate the changes.

Figure 3.19

I have to confirm the changes to my MX records to make them active.

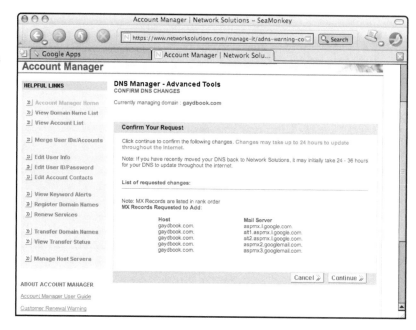

Once I have saved the MX entries for GAYDbook.com at both Network Solutions and in the Google Apps domain alias setup, I am presented with the information screen that you can see in Figure 3.20.

Verifying Domain Aliases

Google Apps is verifying the domain alias by doing its own WHOIS lookup on GAYDbook.com.

Google determines whether the MX records have been properly added to the public DNS record for that domain. The fact that the MX records exist is enough proof for Google to know I own and actually operate the domain in question.

The speed at which Google can verify the domain alias is dependent upon the speed at which your domain registrar–in my case Network Solutions–sends out an update to refresh your WHOIS information.

In my experience, this MX verification process via WHOIS can take anywhere from seconds to several hours. I have never had to wait longer than a day to verify a new domain alias for my Google Apps setup.

GAYDbook.com has been added to my list of domain aliases, and Google Apps informs me that my domain is updating and that it could take up to 48 hours for the process to be complete.

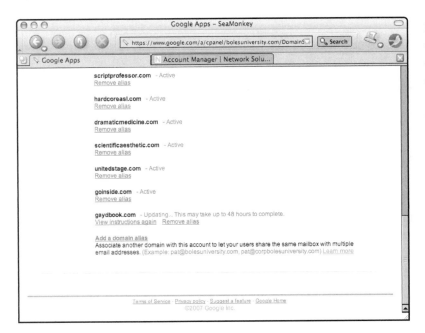

Figure 3.20
Google has to verify the changes you made to your domain's DNS zone file before accepting the new domain alias.

Adding Another Domain Alias

While I'm waiting for GAYDbook.com to get MX verification, I want to add a second domain I registered just for this book: GAPEbook.com—Google Apps Premier Edition Dot Com—so that you can send email to david@gapebook.com if you have a specific question about the Premier Edition of Google Apps!

I also point http://gapebook.com to mask http://bolesbooks.com/thomson so you can visit the homepage for this book using that URL, too!

In Figure 3.21, I enter gapebook.com as another domain alias, and I click on the Continue and Set Up Email Delivery button. For the first time ever, I get an ugly red error message telling me that "This domain has already reached the maximum number of aliases."

Gah!

What?

I am not happy!

I thought the limit for domain aliases was 30, but I guess the limit is more like 20. Things change, and wonders never cease when you're dealing with Google Apps.

Instead of fighting the red stop phrase, I guess I have to delete an already established and verified domain alias. I'll lose my email for that account in my Google Apps Gmail, but if I want to add GAPEbook.com to get mail, I have no other choice but to surrender to the ripping process of the Google gods.

Figure 3.21
Google won't let me add GAPEbook.com as another domain alias! I have to delete another domain alias first before I can continue.

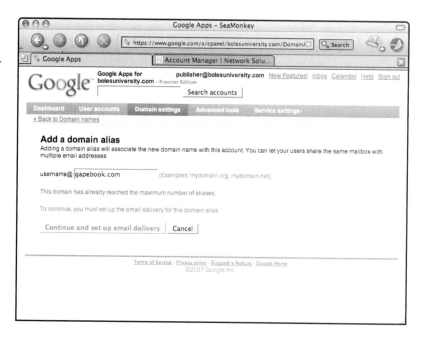

As I begrudgingly poll through my beautiful list of domain aliases, I am left with a sickening stomach and a broken heart as I decide to click on the Remove Alias link under my beloved CitySemiotic.com domain alias to cull it from my Google Apps service, as demonstrated in Figure 3.22.

Google warns me about removing the domain alias, and when I steel myself to the decision, I click on the Yes, Remove Alias button. CitySemiotic.com is banished forever.

Now I have to go all the way back over to Network Solutions, log in to the Advanced Tools DNS Manager, and perform the reverse operation for CitySemiotic.com that I just did for GAYDbook.com.

Instead of adding the Google Apps MX records, I delete them from the CitySemiotic.com DNS zone file and confirm their complete removal by clicking on the Continue button, as evidenced in Figure 3.23.

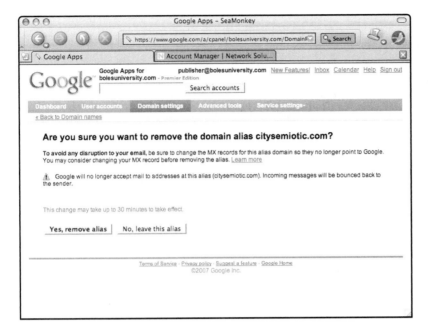

Figure 3.22
I am now removing a domain alias I previously set up.

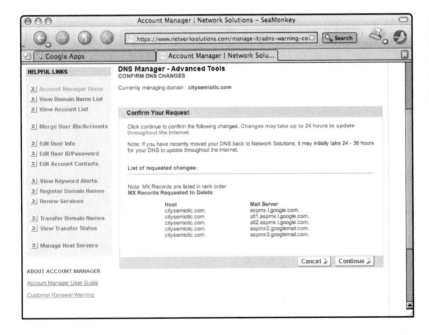

Figure 3.23
I have removed the Google Apps MX records from my CitySemiotic.com DNS zone file.

Updating, Waiting, and Troubleshooting

I bounce back over to my Google Apps Dashboard, go back into my Domain Aliases page, and then add GAPEbook.com as a domain alias. I enter that information into my Network Solutions domain alias as well; when I'm all finished, I get to sit back and wait for Google to verify and update those domain aliases, as seen in Figure 3.24.

> **Tip**
> In order to change the status of your domain alias verification from Updating to Active, you need to keep forcing a refresh on your domain alias page in your Web browser. Press Shift+Refresh/Reload on your keyboard to do so.

Figure 3.24
Both GAYDbook.com and GAPEbook.com are now entered as domain aliases, and they await Google Apps verification.

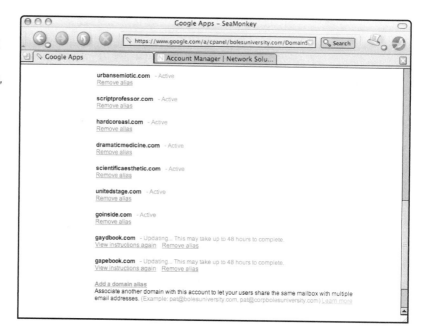

I am an impatient person, and I immediately forced a refresh of my domain alias page. Now GAPEbook.com is active, but GAYDbook.com is still updating, as indicated in Figure 3.25. I find that strange since there was a 30-minute delay between setting up GAYDbook.com, deleting CitySemiotic.com, and setting up GAPEbook.com.

I waited another hour, and GAYDbook.com was still in the Updating stage. This means, in my experience, that something is wonky wrong, because verifying a domain alias usually takes less than a couple of minutes.

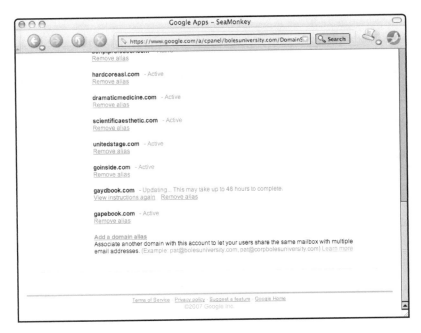

Figure 3.25
GAPEbook.com is now an
active domain alias.

I go back into my Network Solutions DNS Manager to check my MX records for GAYDbook.com. All the entries look correct.

I try a troubleshooting trick by changing one MX entry, making it momentarily incorrect and then saving it. I then wait a minute and change the incorrect MX entry back to the correct setting. I re-save my Network Solutions page of mail server records to force Network Systems to refresh and update the new MX settings for that domain.

I wait 12 minutes to see whether my troubleshooting trick worked.

As you can see in Figure 3.26, my trick worked because all the MX records for GAYDbook.com are now showing up live in a CentralOps.Net WHOIS search.

Caution
The temptation while waiting for this verification is to get angry and impatient and to blame Google, the gods, the world, and anyone in the Google Apps Group who might help you. I caution you that these matters can take time, so don't lose your mind if you have to wait a bit for an update. I am an impatient person, and if I had waited the 48 hours for Google to update my GAYDbook.com domain alias, I'm sure the domain would have eventually been verified because all my entries turned out to be correct. However, I had to check my MX settings anyway just to make sure I didn't make a small mistake. While I was over there checking the entries, it seemed natural and easy to get Network Solutions to update my DNS zone file by making a modification/correction that required a forced save of the changes.

Figure 3.26
A WHOIS search reveals my MX troubleshooting trick worked. All my Google Apps MX records are now live.

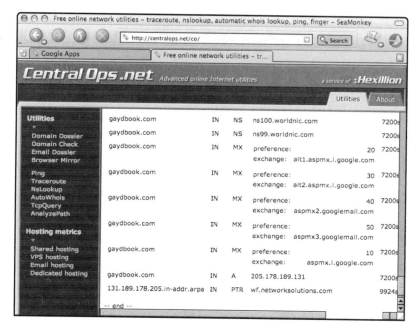

A Dashing Domain

Back in the main Dashboard view, you can see that GAYDbook.com and GAPEbook.com are now listed as active domain aliases under Boles University; see Figure 3.27. That's good news because it means email will start flowing into the inbox for those domains now.

> **Tip**
>
> I will send test messages from my FastMail.FM account to both david@gaydbook.com and david@gapebook.com to make sure the email addresses are active, alive, and able to process inbound email messages. I want to use a secondary email address beyond my Google Apps Gmail to make sure the "outside world" can communicate with the MX servers I set up. I will also reply to those test email messages to make sure the process of sending out mail is working as well.

It was a long, hot road to get here and get them active, but I can now receive mail at both of the new domains via the main BolesUniversity.com Google Apps Gmail account. That's pretty slick!

Before I close this chapter, I want you to look in the upper-right corner of your main Dashboard view and click on the New Features! link.

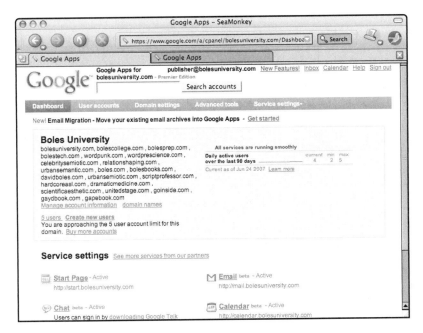

Figure 3.27
GAYDbook.com and
GAPEbook.com are now
listed as active domain
aliases.

The New Features! link is important to check on a regular basis because you will find the latest changes and additions to the Google Apps service. Figure 3.28 shows what happens when you check out new features: Hot news about the new ability to share address books is provided. Sometimes you won't find out about new features on your own or in email. The New Features! link is an invaluable ally for getting the best experience out of Google Apps on a refreshing, ongoing, basis.

Dominating the Dashboard

In this chapter, you've had a chance to become familiar with the Dashboard and its power and functionality! You learned about creating effective logos for privately branding your Google Apps service. You were able to ban all advertising from your Google Apps service and discovered how to be available to end users as the contact administrator.

You also learned how to add a great depth of functionality to your primary domain by adding domain aliases.

In the next chapter, you'll add users to your Google Apps domain and learn how to configure the hidden power of Gmail in order to collaborate online with other users and clients.

Figure 3.28
Frequently check the New
Features! link to get
updated news on Google
Apps features.

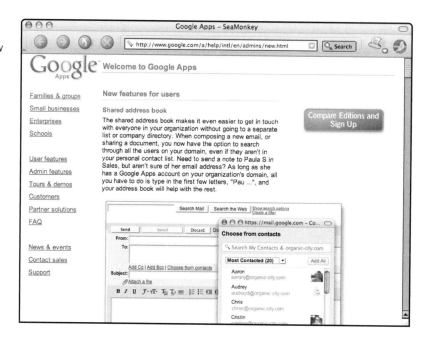

4 Connecting Your Domain Users

In this chapter–the biggest, largest, and most filling chapter of all–you will add users to your domain and learn how to manage them, add them, suspend them, and even delete them! Even if you are your only user, you will find great value in manipulating specific settings of Google Apps Gmail branded with your domain. You will also learn about usernames, aliases, and creating email lists. As well, you will configure your mail options and add another CNAME to your DNS zone file in order to give your email a private label brand.

Heading into the Hole

It's time to head into the *hole*. I call this part of the Google Apps Control Panel where you set up your users the hole because you can easily get lost and confused when it comes to implementing changes from the default Google Apps setup. The first rule of holes–when you find yourself standing in one–is to stop digging. You might be overwhelmed by the possibilities and information in this chapter, and that's okay. Just remember to breathe, read the page again, and pause a moment. You'll soon realize that you're climbing out of the hole and not sinking yourself in deeper.

BlackBerry Access

Figure 4.1 is the login screen for my mail, but before you log in and get heavy into setting up other users, I want to show you that Google Apps supports BlackBerry devices with a special program you download online from http://m.google.com/a. I use this program all the time to check my email via my BlackBerry. It adds great functionality between your BlackBerry and Google Apps that you can't get with the regular Google Apps Web interface through a browser.

Figure 4.1

Google Apps supports BlackBerry email integration with a special program you can download from the Google Web site.

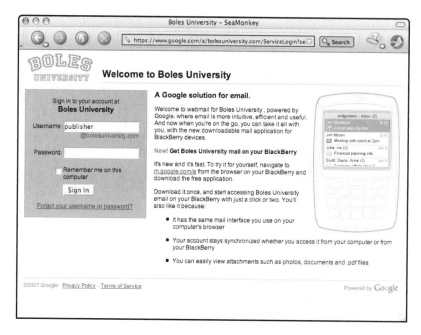

Tip

For fastest BlackBerry interaction with the Google Apps Gmail service, choose More and then Settings from the Sticky menu on your BlackBerry. You should make sure all these options are checked: Always Keep Me Signed In; Preload Messages and Check Mail in the Background for Faster Access, and Use Small Fonts. When you're finished making changes, make sure you save your settings from the Sticky menu.

More Mobile Access

If you don't have a BlackBerry device, you can still log in to your Google Apps Gmail using your cellular phone or PDA by using this direct URL: http://mail.google.com/a/bolesuniversity.com. Just be sure to replace bolesuniversity.com with the name of your own domain.

A Note on Ugly Logins

Google Apps provides neat sub-domain Web addresses you can set up using a CNAME entry such as, say, http://mail.bolesuniversity.com, so you can go right to that Web address to log in to your email system. That Web address makes you look special and professional. You'll set up a mail sub-domain like that later in the chapter.

Of Pretty Logos and Private Labels

However, what Google doesn't really make clear is that your special, private label login URL is pretty much there for show only. The moment you try to access http://mail.bolesuniversity.com, you are immediately redirected to this incredibly ugly and long and atrocious login URL, where you actually enter your username and password:

https://www.google.com/a/bolesuniversity.com/ServiceLogin?service =mail&passive=true&rm=false&continue=http%3A%2F%2Fmail.google.com %2Fa%2Fbolesuniversity.com&ltmpl=default&ltmplcache=2

Why does Google change your URL like that?

One word: security.

Notice that the long and ugly URL starts with "https," which means your login is secured via HTTPS. In order for your domain to have a secure login URL, you would need a security certificate for your domain to enable HTTPS. That can get expensive and complicated, so Google lets you and your users use their HTTPS certificate and secure login instead.

> **Note**
> HTTPS means *Hypertext Transfer Protocol* with the added security of SSL encryption. When you do online banking or log in to PayPal or do other private business online, you are likely in an HTTPS session that is private between you and the entity you're dealing with online.

Of Firewalls and Heartache

You might have some end users who try your special login URL but cannot get into their mail. The problem they are likely encountering is they are on a network that does not like how Google redirects the URL and turns into their long and ugly URL. That sort of redirect from one domain to another can be another sign of phishing, discussed in Chapter 2. For this reason, some computers block these redirection attempts

One workaround is to simply provide your users with the ugly, long, sub-domain URL created by Google. That way, users can head directly into Google without using a "suspicious" URL redirection.

You don't have to give your users that entirely ugly URL. You can shorten and sweeten it some by giving them this much of it:

https://www.google.com/a/bolesuniversity.com/ServiceLogin?service=mail

If you don't give them the "ServiceLogin?service=mail" part of the URL, they will be taken to your Administrator login screen, which probably isn't the safest approach.

> **Caution**
>
> Beware that even that shortened, ugly, login URL might not work on some network systems that are really locked down. To guard against unwanted employee email manipulation and access, some companies and systems choose to block all access to the Google domain. That means users can't get into anything Google related–including your Google Apps hosted domain.

Of Always Forcing HTTPS and Security

There is a keen trick you can use to force a secure HTTPS session for your Google Apps hosted experience. This trick involves creating links or saving bookmarks to the various long, ugly URLs instead of the pretty sub-domain–specific URLs that point to your domain.

On the main http://bolesuniverisity.com page, you will see links under the Boles University logo to Mail, Calendar, Docs, and Start. Each of those links goes to the long URL for the service, with one special addition that I made. Instead of just saving the long URL as an http:// address, I added an "S" to the "HTTP" to guarantee all Google Apps logins are on the Google secure HTTPS server. Working under https:// instead of http:// means you are always under a Google-protected private session where other thieving eyes cannot spy.

> **Tip**
>
> Unfortunately, the HTTPS trick won't work with your customized, domain-specific, Google Apps start page. If you add an "S" to your HTTP address for your start page, you will instead be redirected to the plain old generic Google search page we have all come to know and love. You cannot access the start page via a secure connection. Google does that because you will likely add widgets and other features–you'll do that in Chapter 7–outside of the Google domain, which means Google cannot verify, control, or secure the content. Therefore, your Google Apps URL will not load via a secure connection.

Into the Email!

Now you're ready to log in to the Control Panel so you can start to customize your email and add your users. As you can see in Figure 4.2, the dynamic graph you've seen in previous chapters is empty because the Active Users graph did not load. This happens quite a lot in Google Apps, and while it is disappointing, it doesn't have any effect on your Google Apps interface or domain functionality. Click on Advanced Tools in the Dashboard view to get things really rolling!

Figure 4.2
The Active Users graph might not always be available. Stay Tuned means that this time, the graph is not available.

Manipulating Advanced Tools

Advanced Tools is the best place to start to get your domain users ingested into Google Apps. You'll take a quick tour through this page found in Figure 4.3. You won't learn how to manipulate every option on this page because some of it is too specific and involves too many conditions and options that I can't begin to cover here. Click on User Accounts Bulk Update to start a bulk upload of your current user base.

Bulk Upload Users

If you have your users in a CSV file, Google Apps makes it easy to bring them all into your domain with a single button click to upload the file. Figure 4.4 shows you that Google even provides a graphic example of the format it needs for your users to be found in your file.

You can create new accounts through this method or update existing accounts and even require a password change for all uploaded users.

Figure 4.3
This is the Advanced Tools
page, where you can set
the parameters of your
Google Apps service.

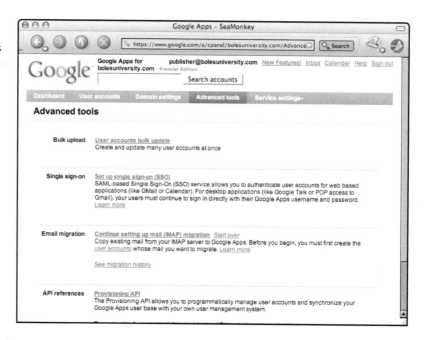

> **Note**
> Gmail and Google Apps Mail (your branded Gmail) are slightly different. Usernames can use letters
> (a–z) and numbers (0–9) and dashes (-) and periods. Google Apps Mail, unlike regular Gmail, accepts
> dots (.) in usernames. That means "davidboles" and "david.boles" are two separate users on Google
> Apps, whereas in regular Gmail, david.boles@gmail.com and davidboles@gmail.com are the same
> address. Regular Gmail doesn't see the dot between the names, so it is only an aesthetic function and
> not a differentiating one.

Setting a Single Sign-On

Enabling a single sign-on (SSO) is a complicated process for advanced domain administrators,
and because every company is different, I have no way of cohesively demonstrating here how
to set up the service for you. Figure 4.5 indicates the parameters you need to set in order to get
SSO working with your site. You're making Google more of a service provider than an authen-
tication host for your domain. The link to the SSO Reference on that setup page will give you
all the details you need to enable this feature for your domain.

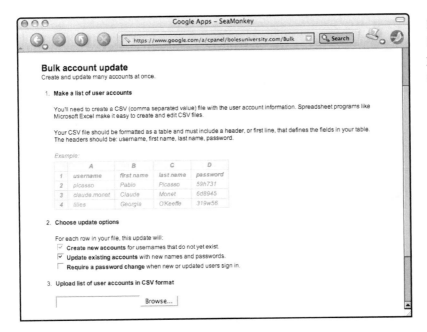

Figure 4.4
Bulk Account Update lets you create or update your users using a CSV file.

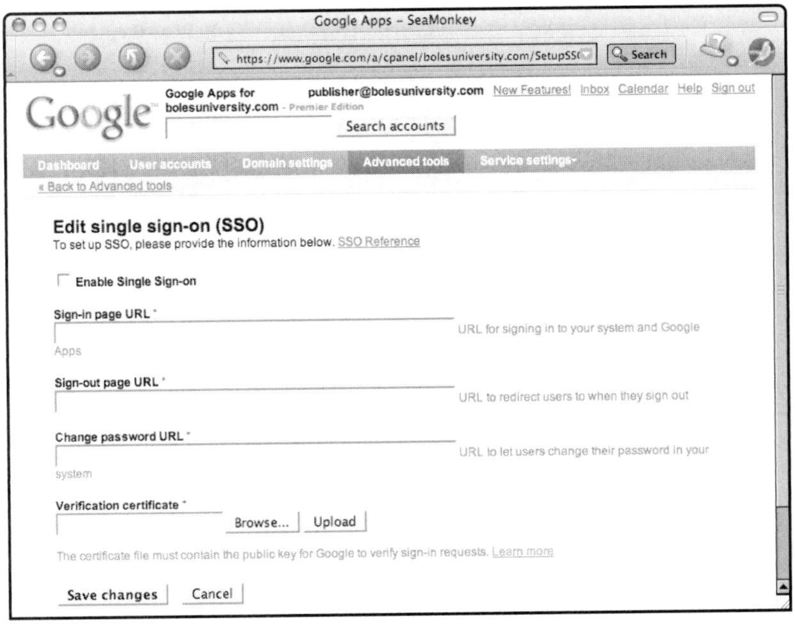

Figure 4.5
If you prefer to authenticate your users for all services with a single sign-on, you can set up that feature on this page.

Easy IMAP Email Migration

Google makes it easy to move all your email from your current email into Google Apps. Your migrated email will retain its original sender information, including the date the email was originally received and not the import/migration date. The "read" status of your old mail will also be preserved when it's pulled into your new Google Apps mail. Once all your email is migrated, Google Apps will map your folders to Gmail labels and thread all your conversations. You'll be able to search all your old mail with the great Google search capability. You can migrate one user or many.

> **Note**
> Central Piedmont Community College migrated 30,000 users in three weeks. Three million email messages were migrated from the old email server into Google Apps in under 24 hours. That breaks down to over 2,000 emails migrating per minute!

Connecting to Your Remote Email Server

The first step in migrating your email is to connect to your remove IMAP server. You need to fill in some specific information that you will need to look up and enter on your end, as shown in Figure 4.6. You can set the number of allowed connections to your server and even add a blackout time so you don't migrate during the busy morning weekday work hours.

Figure 4.6

The first step in migrating your old email is to tell Google Apps where to find your old mail.

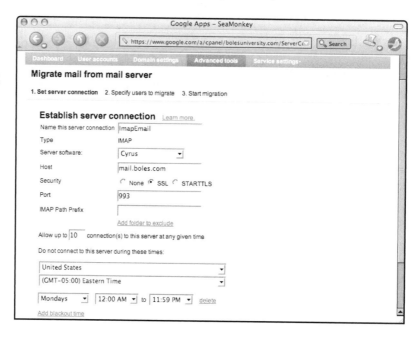

Picking Users

Next, you need to specify the users to migrate. This is a simple process of providing a few names or uploading a file with thousands of usernames, as shown in Figure 4.7. When you're ready to start the email migration, click on the Continue button.

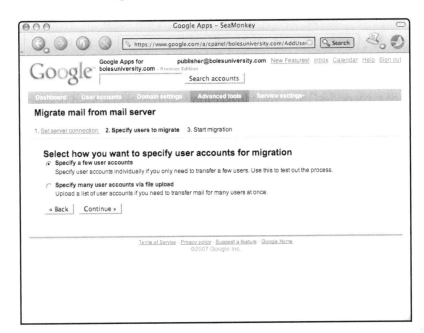

Figure 4.7

Now you need to tell Google Apps which users you want to migrate.

Start Me Up!

You're almost there! Figure 4.8 indicates the users I want to move over from my old IMAP system. I'm moving only a few users, so I'm not uploading a file. When I'm ready to transfer everyone, I just need to click on the Test Connection button and the email will be ready to fly!

> **Note**
> *Source username* is the username on the old email system. Your Google Apps username and the source username do not have to be identical for the migration to happen.

Figure 4.8

Click the Test Connection button to begin the email migration.

Coding GData API References

The final option listed on your Advanced Tools page is API References. You can write your own user database management with the Google Data (GData) API. I won't get into that now because that's a whole book unto itself. I'm mentioning it now, though, to make you aware of it and to let you know I didn't actually forget about this feature. If you want the lowdown on the guts of the Google GData API references, check out this site for more info: http://code.google.com/apis/gdata/reference.html.

This feature is available only in the Google Apps Premier Edition and the Google Apps Education Edition.

General Email Settings

Now let's go back to the Dashboard view in your Control Panel. Near the middle of the page, find the Email icon under the Service Settings heading and click on it. You will be taken to the settings page for your email, where there's lots of deep-level interaction you can set up, as indicated in Figure 4.9.

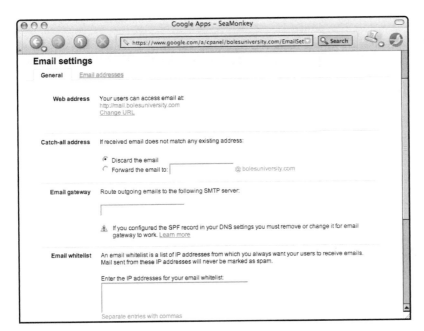

Figure 4.9
This is the General Email Settings page, where you can determine your email experience.

Branding Your Mail URL

You can set up a sub-domain Web address for Google Apps by clicking on the Change URL link, as shown in Figure 4.10. I prefer the descriptive default http://mail.bolesuniversity.com, but some people want an even shorter URL like http://m.bolesuniversity.com. You can make your sub-domain anything you wish. Just enter your choice in the text field and click the Continue button. You can also change the URLs for all Google Apps domain services from this page.

You will need to edit your DNS zone file to make the CNAME sub-domain change active. I covered changing CNAMEs in Chapters 2 and 3 with lots of visual steps to follow. Here's a quick reminder how to create a new CNAME record for your mail sub-domain.

1. Sign in to your Web host or domain registrar so you can change your DNS entries.

2. Enter mail as the CNAME value or alias.

3. Make ghs.google.com. the CNAME address or destination. Don't forget to add the dot (period) at the end of the entry!

4. Save the changes to your DNS zone file.

5. Click on the I've Completed These Steps button on the Changing CNAME Record page in your email settings interface to confirm the modification.

In a few hours, your new CNAME entry should be updated and then will propagate across the Internet.

Figure 4.10

Brand your email URL on
this page.

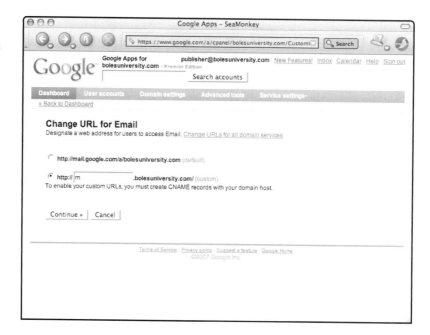

Grabbing Odd Mail

Back on the General Email Settings page, you can also add a catch-all address for your domain.
I call this *odd mail* because it is mail sent to you that doesn't match a currently active user
account. Many times odd mail is just spam, and that's why I don't like to use a catch-all address,
but if you want to monitor mail sent to a suspended or deleted user, the catch-all method can
be a good way to silently manage that duty.

If you decide to implement a catch-all address, be sure you add an email address for your domain
and save the information.

> **Caution**
> Beware that creating a catch-all address will bring you tons of spam, and so you might want to create
> a filter, or a special email address or email alias, that will catch that spam and keep it away from your
> real administrator email address. That way, you can keep an eye on the caught messages without
> overwhelming your inbox with spam.

Use Your Own SMTP Server

If you do not want to use the Google servers to send your mail, you can enter your own email
gateway for sending mail. Just enter the SMTP server address and save the page.

Tip

If you change your email gateway and choose to create a DNS zone entry for your SPF records, as discussed in Chapter 2, you need to remove the SPF record because it points to the Google mail servers and not the server you intend to use.

Vouching for IP Addresses

Google Apps also lets you enter "trusted" IP addresses in the General Email Settings page so you can white-list trusted mail servers. You must know the IP address of the mail server you want to white-list. You do not enter individual email addresses in the text box or domain names. You enter IP addresses to white-list, separated by commas. White-listed IP addresses will never be marked as spam by Google Apps.

No Mail, Thank You!

If you need to disable the Google Apps email, you can scroll to the bottom of the General Email Settings and choose to stop the email service. You might need to do that for a troubleshooting reason, or you might want to use a different, unsupported, email system apart from what Google Apps offers. The choice is yours. You can re-enable mail just as easily by reversing the step you chose to turn it off.

Email Addresses

Now it's time to manage email addresses. On your Email Settings page, click on the Email Addresses link. You'll see all your current email addresses, the ability to create an email list, and any nicknames you may have already created. If you haven't set any nicknames yet, we'll do that together soon.

The first email list you see is called abuse@bolesuniversity.com, and I'm going to click on the 2 Recipient link in the Recipients column, as seen in Figure 4.11.

Alerting Abuse and Postmaster

The Google team plays big brother in one big way when it comes to helping you manage your email. Google monitors the required "abuse@" and "postmaster@" email addresses for your domain. If someone complains about you, about your site, or about someone from your site sending out unwanted spam, people will use those two addresses to find you, when in reality they are tattling directly to Google by default without your direct knowledge or feedback or participation.

The way to at least be part of the complaint loop is to create an email list called "abuse" and "postmaster" and add yourself as one of the recipients!

Figure 4.11
This is the Email Addresses page, where you can view all your current addresses and create an email list.

You can see my abuse@bolesuniversity.com in Figure 4.12. Google Support is already there by default and cannot be removed. By adding my email address, I will at least see who is complaining about me and the what and why of the complaint in case Google chooses to find me and ask me about the complaints.

I have also created a postmaster@bolesuniversity.com email list with Google Support and myself as the only recipients. If you have more than one administrator for your domain, you can add them to your email list as well. You can even add email recipients outside your hosted domain in case you want to use a separate email account to monitor these reports.

Note
You can also create a filter for the "abuse" and "postmaster" email lists for your domain in your Google Apps mail. I filter those emails into "xAbuse" and "xPostmaster" labels, and I added the "x" to the front of those words to make sure they appear at the bottom of my labels list. I have yet to deal with any email on those lists, and the further out of sight, the better out of mind.

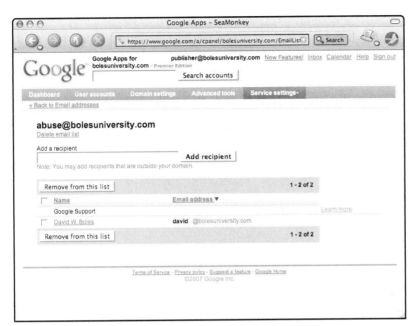

Figure 4.12
Create an "abuse" email
list to monitor complaints
against your Google Apps
domain.

Populating Your Own Lists

It's time to create an email list of your own by clicking on the Back to Email Addresses link and choosing Create an Email List. As demonstrated in Figure 4.13, I have decided to create an email list called GAYDreaders, and I have added a recipient. I can choose to add one email address at a time, or I can gang add every single person in my domain. Once you choose to add one person to a list, your list is alive and functioning. Any email sent to GAYDreaders@bolesuniversity.com will immediately be forwarded to everyone on that list.

> **Caution**
> Email lists can easily be abused by those who know their special addresses. Google protects you—as the domain owner and administrator—from your own users by allowing only administrators to send mail to email lists created using the Add Everyone in My Domain option.

When your email list is created, you are presented with a confirmation screen, as seen in Figure 4.14. This screen provides the finished email address for the email list. You see the Delete Email List link under the new email list address? You can click on that link to start all over. Let's click on it and see what happens!

Figure 4.13
Creating your own email list is as easy as naming it and adding a recipient.

Figure 4.14
This is the email list confirmation screen, which includes the option to delete the list.

You are presented with a big warning box in red letters in Figure 4.15 asking you if you are certain you want to delete the email list. Google is good about protecting an itchy finger. You are always asked if you really want to do something irreversible. Should you leave that newly created email in place by clicking the Cancel button, or do you want to really delete it? The choice is yours!

Figure 4.15
You can delete your email list or click on the Cancel button to keep the list.

Managing Your Folk

Let's visit your user accounts by clicking on the User Accounts option in the blue menu bar on your Dashboard. I have a big, red warning that reads "You have reached the 5 user account limit for this domain." Note the option to buy more user accounts. As demonstrated in Figure 4.16, you will also see a list of active domain users. You see their names, usernames, status as an administrator or user, their email quota, and most impressively, the last time they signed in to your domain.

Manipulating User Settings

Let's click on the Boles University username and see what options I can set and add to my account. As you can see in the top half of this screen in Figure 4.17, there are many features to manipulate in this individual user screen. I can change the name of Boles University to something else. I can reset a password or require my user to change his or her password on the next login.

I can also choose to allow this user to administrate the entire domain as well as getting a fine overview of all the active domain alias email addresses that you set up in Chapter 3.

Figure 4.16
This Users view is packed with juicy information about the folk in your domain.

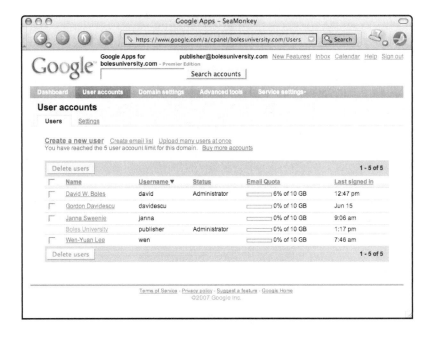

> **Tip**
> Only administrators can reset Google Apps domain passwords. If a user is locked out of his account and needs a new password, only you can get the user back in with a password rescue.

Maintaining Nicknames and Lists

As you scroll down to the bottom half of the user settings page for Boles University in Figure 4.18, you see more active domain alias email addresses and a place where we can add nicknames and add users to email lists. Nicknames are a wondrous thing because they give you new email addresses without having to purchase or add new accounts!

You might want to create a nickname for boss@bolesuniversity.com or books@bolesuniversity.com and then label and filter the mail for special attention.

> **Note**
> Nicknames will work across all your active domain aliases for all your users as well! Messages to boss@gaydbook.com and books@gapebook.com will both arrive in your inbox just like those addressed to "david" will arrive in your inbox from both of those domains.

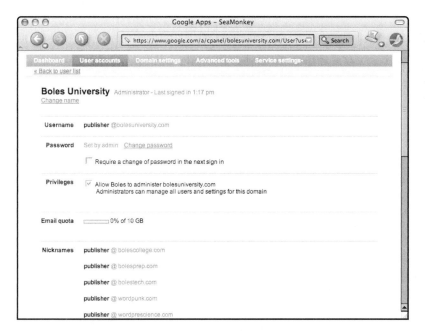

Figure 4.17
This is the top half of the individual administration area for the manipulation of single user settings.

Figure 4.18
This is the bottom half of the individual user settings. Here, you can add nicknames and place users into email lists.

Becoming a Plus Alias

Google Apps has a mysterious limit on the number of nicknames you can create. I hear from other Google Apps domain administrators that the limit ranges anywhere from 30 to 102 but no one–not even Google Support–can really give you a definite answer. The limit seems to vary from domain to domain.

If you run out of nicknames, the easiest way to get more unique addresses is to use *plus aliases*. Aliases are neat, and they work, and you create them on your own. You don't have to tell Google Apps to do anything special to handle those email aliases. No setup is required.

Here's how they work. In Google Apps, the "+" (plus) sign is the key to using a successful alias. Email addressed to david+computer@bolesuniversity.com is delivered to david@bolesuniversity.com. Anything you add after the "+" sign is the plus alias. In my example, the word "computer" is the plus alias because that word appears after the "+" sign.

Plus aliases are an easy way to create a myriad of email addresses you can use to fool spammers. If you use david+bank@bolesuniversity.com to do all your online banking and you get email from your bank at a different address that isn't the private alias you created, you know the email is fake.

There is no limit on the number of plus aliases you can create with Google Apps, so have at it. You can have some fun funneling your mail into specific areas for analysis and responding to others you have "pre-verified" as legitimate because only they have your plus alias address!

Dealing with Problem Users

Sometimes the threats to your domain don't come from the outside. Sometimes the attacks are within your domain and not beyond your domain. Sometimes your users go bad and send spam, get fired, tick you off, or just decide to poop off on their own.

How do you handle problem users?

Picking on Gordon

Go into your User list to find out what options are available to you. Figure 4.19 shows information for end user Gordon Davidescu. Right under his name, you can see we can change his name, suspend him, or delete him forever. Gordon is a big, fun friend of mine, but let's pretend—for now—that he's done something wrong. He's sending out tons of unwanted mail, and he just won't stop.

Caution

Be careful when you delete users because Google imposes a five-day waiting period before you can reactivate a deleted name or service.

Figure 4.19
This is Gordon Davidescu's user information. We can manage his Boles University life right from this screen.

Suspending Gordon

You could just get rid of Gordon and delete him. Gordon is a pretty good guy, though, and if you delete him, you'll have to wait five days before you can add him back to Boles University under the same username.

Let's choose to suspend him instead. When you click on the Suspend User link, the page shown in Figure 4.20 appears and asks whether you really want to suspend the user.

> **Note**
> Suspended users are not deleted, and their information will stay intact, but in stasis. Don't use Suspend to hold new email if you or one of your users goes away on vacation. Suspend is almost delete, but with a reprieve, which you'll see next.

Okay, you suspended Gordon!

Figure 4.21 indicates Gordon is now in Suspended status; it must be cold out there. Under his username we see Suspend User has been replaced with a Restore User link.

Figure 4.20
You can either suspend Gordon or cancel this process and leave his user account active.

Figure 4.21
This screen confirms Gordon's suspension and also provides the means to immediately restore him to full Boles University manhood.

Caution

Email to suspended users does not go into your catch-all address. Email to suspended users gets bounced back to the sender as an invalid email address.

Pardoning Gordon

Let's head back to the User Accounts screen. You can see that Gordon's status has changed to Suspended in the list view of users, so he's officially out in the cold, as Figure 4.22 indicates.

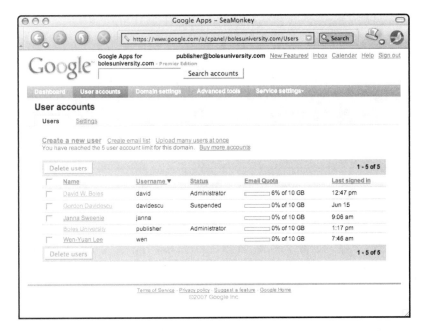

Figure 4.22
This main User Accounts view shows Gordon's status has been changed to Suspended in the list view.

You can click on his name and use the Restore User option to bring him right back to Active status. Let's do just that now, because we generally like Gordon–except when he's a little late on his deadlines–and we want him back in the Boles University fold.

Gordon gets an immediate pardon!

Creating New Users

Now you need to create a new Boles University account for Sarah. She's the newest member of the team, and you need to give her full access to the domain services. Because I'm using the Premier Edition Google Apps plan, I'll need to pony up some dough to Google in order to add her. Let's head back to the Google Apps Dashboard and click on the Buy More Accounts link in the middle of the page to start the process.

Adding Sarah

When you choose to create a new user by buying a new account, you are immediately taken to the Google Checkout interface. In Figure 4.23, you can see the price for adding a new account is $45.76 USD instead of $50.00 USD. Google prorates your yearly subscription so all your user accounts will expire on the same day. That helps you negotiate the easy renewal of all service one time a year. When you're ready to take the next step, press the Proceed to Google Checkout button.

> **Note**
> Many Google Apps Premier Edition users want a "mixed method" of adding users. Some users should be free with a standard 2 gig storage, while other people in the domain need the advantages of the 10 gigs of storage. Google has hinted there may be a way to mix free and paid accounts in the future, so keep an eye open for that lurking possibility coming soon!

Figure 4.23
Tell Google how many extra accounts you want to purchase.

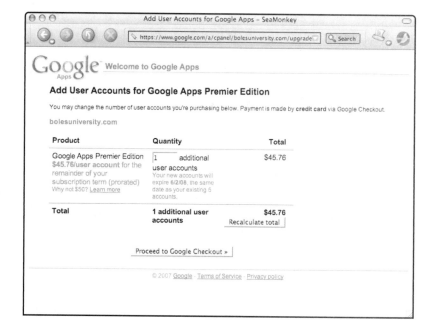

Buying Sarah

The final step in purchasing the new account is to confirm your information with Google Checkout, as indicated in Figure 4.24. If you want to get promotional email from Google Apps, make sure you check the box enabling that feature. I always want email from Google Apps because I get forewarned on new features that are not always visible to my busy eye online. When you're ready to complete your transaction, click the Place Your Order Now button and you're done!

> **Tip**
>
> Make sure you want the new account because you can't get a refund if you change your mind later. You don't have to renew the account in a year, but once you pay for a new account, that account is created with no way to reverse the charges.

Figure 4.24
This is the final confirmation screen for Google Checkout.

Creating Sarah

Okay, now you have a new account ready for Sarah. You have two confirmation emails from Google verifying the purchase and the ability to add a new user. Go to your Google Apps Dashboard and click on the Create New Users link in the middle of the page. You will be presented with a similar screen, seen in Figure 4.25. Enter the appropriate information—you can even create a new password instead of using the auto-generated default created by the Google system—and click the Create New User button.

Figure 4.25
Fill in the information for your new user; you can set a custom password, too.

Confirming Sarah

Sarah is alive! The confirmation screen in Figure 4.26 has all the important information I need to send to Sarah so she can log in and join all our fun. Let's click on the Edit Settings for Sarah link to make sure she's correctly set up in the Google Apps system.

Inviting Sarah

Figure 4.27 belongs to Sarah's user page. You can see she is Newly Created, and she has yet to log in. You could suspend her and even delete her if we're looking for some fun, but we're not. We're all about business at Boles University. You could also give Sarah administrator privileges. Instead, let's choose to click on the Email Instructions link so you can give Sarah a good hearty welcome and provide her password and other pertinent links for interacting with the Google Apps domain.

Figure 4.26
This screen confirms Sarah is now a part of Boles University!

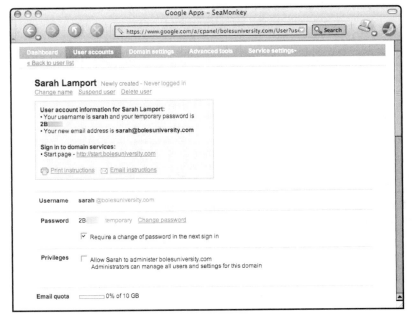

Figure 4.27
You can use this screen to make Sarah an administrator or to email her instructions for logging in to the domain.

Writing an Effective Welcome Letter

The default "welcome letter" Google Apps provides for your new users is a little brief and totally bland. Here's the sort of letter I send to my new users. You're welcome to steal it and use it as you please:

Hi Sarah!

Welcome to Boles University! Here is some information concerning your new Google Apps account at Boles University.

* Your username is "sarah" and your temporary password is _____.

* Your new email address is sarah@bolesuniversity.com.

* You may sign in to our university Start Page at: http://start.bolesuniversity.com.

* You may also find login information at http://bolesuniversity.com.

* Your Boles University email is located at http://mail.bolesuniversity.com.

* Your new Calendar is here: http://calendar.bolesuniversity.com.

* Documents, Spreadsheets, and Presentations may be created here: http://docs.bolesuniversity.com.

You may use this account as your personal account as you wish—your email has 10 gigs of storage!

Your account is private. No one else can see or have access to your mail or other features. You can also have your current email forwarded to this new account if you like.

If you need help with something, feel free to contact us.

Have a wonderful day!

Best Wishes,

David W. Boles

http://BolesUniversity.com

Sarah in Situ

You aren't quite done with Ms. Sarah yet. Let's head into the User Accounts screen so you can see Sarah in situ—in position—along with the rest of the great minds that make up Boles University. There she is, as displayed in Figure 4.28, shining out at us as our newest user in the body of Boles University. If you ever need to make changes to a user account, you just click on the user's name to access the user's settings area.

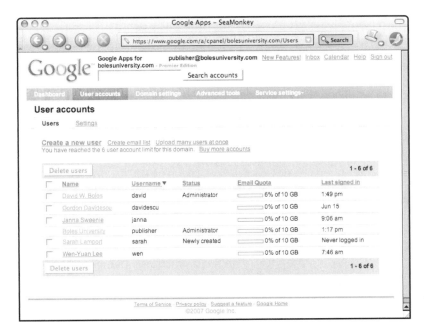

Figure 4.28
Sarah has taken her
rightful position as a new
user at Boles University.

Bah-Ooo-Gah! Google Lockdowns and Limits

You always need to remember your domain is not an island unto itself. You are in business with Google. Google Apps is your online hosting partner. There are certain limitations, restrictions, and lockdowns you need to know about now so you don't get caught and are sorry later. The lockdown warnings are ominous and sort of science-fictiony.

500 per Day Limit

You cannot send more than 500 messages a day on one account via the Google Apps Gmail interface or 100 messages if you use POP access. Period. Those limits include any and all To, CC, and BCC fields. If you do, or if you try to send more than 500/100 emails, Google will automatically lock your account for 24 hours. If you send a lot of messages under those thresholds that are undeliverable, you also risk getting locked out because you may be flagged as a spammer. Email systems automatically assume you are sending email messages to people you know, and if you are getting bounce-backs in large numbers, then something must be awry. Don't let Google think you've gone awry!

> **Tip**
> If you need to communicate with a lot of people, consider using a third-party remailer or start a Google Group of your own to send out blast messages. You can even create private Google groups. For more information on starting a Google Group, go to http://groups.google.com.

Lockdown in Sector 4

If your account is marked with a "Lockdown in Sector 4," that might mean Google has detected abnormal activity on your account, so you are closed down for 24 hours. If you send 500 emails or continuously refresh your browser interface, you can get locked down. This is the message from Google you might see:

> "Our system indicates unusual usage of your account. In order to protect Gmail users from potentially harmful use of Gmail, this account has been disabled for up to 24 hours.

> If you are using any third-party software that interacts with your Gmail account, please disable it or adjust it so that its use complies with the Gmail Terms of Use. If you feel that you have been using your Gmail account according to the Terms of Use or otherwise normally, please contact us at gmail-lockdown@google.com to report this problem."

Note

When Google mentions "any third-party software" as a possible cause for your Sector 4 lockdown, one thing they may be wondering about is if you are trying to use your Google Apps Gmail as a hard drive to store files. There are programs available from third parties that violate the Google Terms of Use by giving you access to your Gmail account as if it were a virtual disk instead of an email account. I'm not going to mention the names of any of those programs, because if you have no idea what I'm talking about, that's a good way of protecting you from a Google lockdown.

Problems in Sector Five

If you get "Sector 5" bounces from Google, that can mean you are sending mail that is not getting received, and your messages are beginning to bounce back in a quantity that may lead you into a lockdown in Sector 4. Why does a Sector 5 warning come before a Sector 4 lockdown? I have no idea! I do know this, though: Consider yourself warned in a Sector 5 environment. If you're in the middle of a massive email blast, stop it. Disconnect from the Gmail email server and be proactive in locking yourself down in whatever sector makes sense to you.

Lockdown in Sector 6

Lockdowns in Sector 6 are pretty rare. It appears Sector 6 lockdowns are triggered by a large number of Gmail accounts that have been registered and then rendered as igniters of spam. It seems Google proactively works to shut down that kind of mass attack from within their system by disabling all suspicious user accounts that have personality imprints that match the propagation attack. You might get caught in that Google wrath, and you will be unable to view attachments, download attachments, or forward messages for 24 hours or so. You can always appeal to Google directly—you will be provided with an online form to fill in if you get a Sector 6 lockdown—but you should be able to read, send, and receive your mail.

Presenting Contacts

One of the coolest things about Google Apps is the ability to share contacts among users in your domain. To enable this feature, go into User Accounts and then choose Settings and click the button that says Enable Contact Sharing; see Figure 4.29. You may enable the provisioning API on this page–that's too advanced and variously specific for this book–and you may also enable the single sign-on feature discussed earlier in this chapter.

> **Caution**
>
> It can take up to 30 minutes for contact sharing to propagate across your domain. Don't go crazy wondering why the feature isn't working right away. Give it some time to set up. Then log out and back in again to your Google Apps Gmail to see the power of the feature.

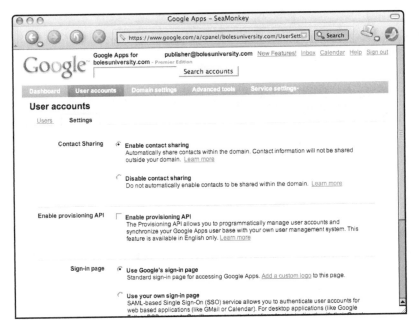

Figure 4.29
You can enable contact sharing across your domain.

Priming Contacts

In your Google Apps Gmail view, choose the Compose Mail option in the left sidebar and then, as shown in Figure 4.30, look for the new Choose from Contacts link that has now magically appeared under the To address window. That link is now available because you enabled it for your users in the Google Apps Dashboard. Click on the link to start a user search based on your domain!

Figure 4.30

You have a new feature, the Choose from Contacts option located under the To address window.

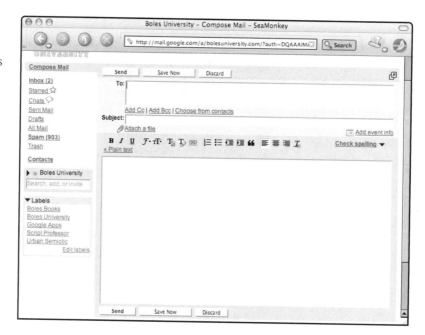

Parsing Contacts

A Choose from Contacts window will appear, and in the first search box you will see Search My Contacts & Boles University. The extra & Boles University is the proof your domain-wide Google Apps contacts sharing is enabled and working, as shown in Figure 4.31.

> **Tip**
>
> Only the "bolesuniversity.com" usernames are shared. If you have private contacts in your contact list, those private contacts will remain private.

Picking Contacts

Now I will look for my newest user, Sarah, by typing her name in my search window. (Even though she was already in my original list, play along with me now.) When I click on Sarah's name, she is highlighted, and a green check appears next to her name, as in Figure 4.32. I can choose to create a mailing group or click on the Done button to begin composing a letter to Sarah. I'm done!

> **Note**
>
> Searching for users when Contact Sharing is enabled does not give you the opportunity to search based on your domain name. For example, I cannot enter "bolesuniversity," "bolesuniversity.com," or "*.bolesuniversity.com" in the search box and get all the users in my domain to load. I can search for contacts—private or shared—by typing in usernames only.

Prodding Contacts

Now I can present Sarah with my offer in email in Figure 4.33. Sarah has been auto-added in my To window, and I only have to worry about composing an effective commentary in my message window. When I'm ready, all I need to do is click Send and I can make my offer!

Figure 4.32
I clicked on Sarah's name to choose her as my email recipient.

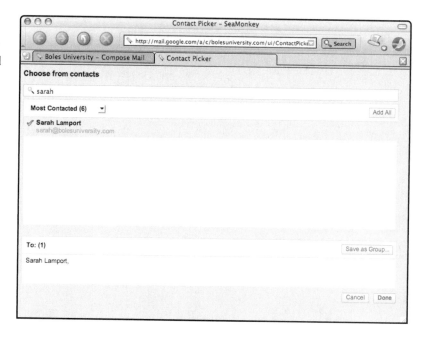

Figure 4.33
Choosing to email contacts from within your own domain is a simple synchronization.

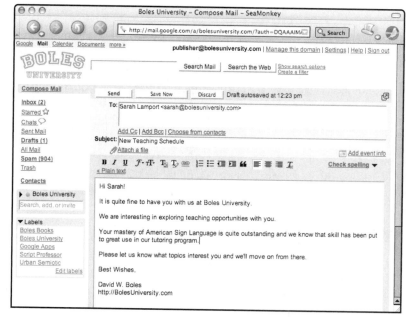

Sending from Different Accounts

One of the greatest features of adding domain aliases to Google Apps, as you learned in Chapter 3, is the ability to then send email from those associate domains from your Gmail Web interface. You can receive mail from those domain aliases, but you are not yet able to send mail as a user of those domain aliases. Setting up those alternative email accounts can be a little confusing because there are several intricate, necessary steps you must take to add the new domain as a verified email account. You'll learn how to do all of that next.

Adding Account Super Powers!

To begin sending mail via your Google Apps domain alias, you need to first log in to your Google Apps Gmail. Then, as demonstrated in Figure 4.34 (where you can see the top half of my ongoing list of verified domain aliases for sending mail), click on the Settings link in the upper-right corner of your screen and choose Accounts from the available list of options

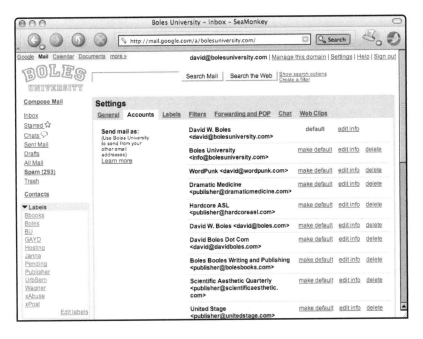

Figure 4.34
Send mail using a domain alias by manipulating your Settings screen.

Including Another Email Address

Next you need to head to the bottom half of the Accounts screen. Figure 4.35 indicates where you can choose to reply from the same address your domain alias email was sent to, or you can always reply from your default email address. Because all of my domains are aliased with Google Apps, I like to reply from the same address the message was sent to. This option gives me a wider communication stretch under one email interface. I can interact with anyone trying to reach me via a specific email address other than my main Boles University account.

> **Caution**
>
> When you are working with your account settings, you want to choose the option Add Another Mail Account when you're working with verified domain aliases. You need to add another email address to send via your new domain alias instead of just receiving mail.

Figure 4.35

Choose to add another email address if you want to send mail from a domain alias.

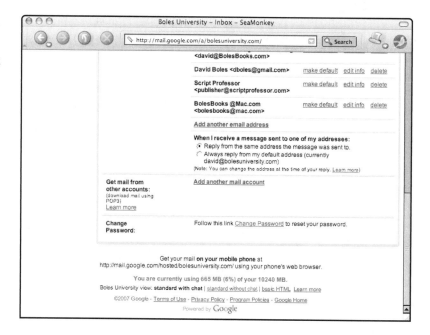

Tapping the Address

When you click on the Add Another Email Account link, you will be presented with the screen in Figure 4.36, where you will need to insert your name and the email address from which you wish to send mail. I'm adding david@gaydbook.com to my account. You need to use this process every time you add a new email address from which you want to send mail.

> **Tip**
>
> You can use this method to reply from an email account that is not a domain alias just as long as you can tell Google Apps that you are the owner of the mail account.

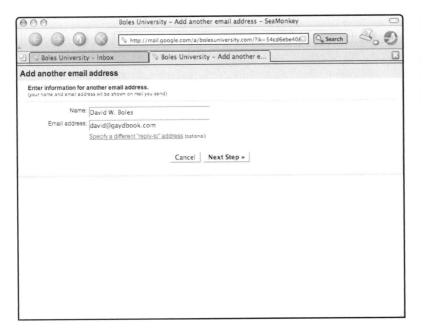

Figure 4.36
Enter the information for the email address from which you intend to send mail.

Verifying Who You Are... AGAIN?

What can I say? It's verification time again! When you're setting up your Google Apps domain, you will need to confirm you are authorized to do what you want to do each step of the way. The good news is that, once you successfully verify all your features, you won't have to verify any of them again unless you change or remove the feature. The bad news is that you need to do a little more verification; just keep in mind that Google is big on security and account identity. Click the Send Verification button shown in Figure 4.37 to begin the verification process.

Re-Re-Confirming Your Identity

In my experience, Google will quickly—within seconds—verify your identity with an email sent to the new account. When that verification email arrives, you need to either enter the confirmation code included in your Google account setup or, easier yet, just click on the provided link, as shown in Figure 4.38.

Successful as Superman!

When you click the confirmation link in your verification email—try saying that three times fast!—you will be taken to a Confirmation Success! screen. You might feel faster than a speeding bullet and more powerful than a locomotive as you realize Superman has nothing on your amazing feats of communication strength!

Figure 4.37

Google needs to verify that you own and can respond from the email account you are trying to add.

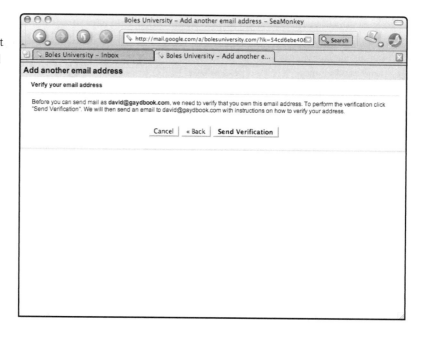

Figure 4.38

This is the confirmation email you must respond to in order to verify that you own the email account you are adding.

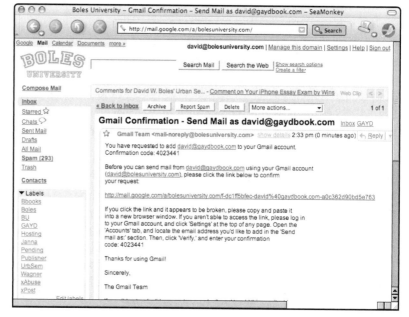

Figure 4.39
Google has confirmed
your new account as valid!

Trust, But Verify

Okay, so Google ran you through the wringer! Now it's your turn to repay the favor with a few twists. Google confirmed your new email account as valid, and all is right with the world, right?

Wrong!

Now you must test Google. You need to determine whether Google is set up to actually send and accept mail from your newly created account. This is an important step that some people forget until it's too late and they're under a critical deadline. The process is straightforward and simple if you take the time to accurately reproduce all the steps.

Go into your Google Apps Gmail, click on the Compose Mail link in the left sidebar, and then click on the down arrow in the From area to reveal, in my case, a long list of verified domain aliases.

Figure 4.40 demonstrates all the From addresses I have verified with Google Apps. I need to scroll down to the middle of my Accounts list to select the email account I added: david@gaydbook.com. Then I'll send a test message to another account I own that is separate from Google Apps to make sure the email address is valid both coming and going.

Figure 4.40

Select the new account you added so you can send mail from it to another account. This process tests if the new email address is working.

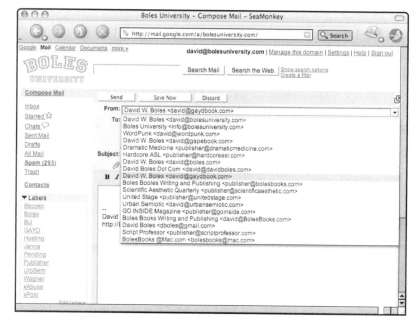

A Sidebar on Behalf of a Sidebar

Despite your best intentions to send mail from a unique email account domain alias you successfully added and verified, there are some email programs out there–the most widely used is Microsoft Outlook–that will rat you out and note that you are not who you are pretending to be in your email response.

I call this "The Curse of the On Behalf Of Curse."

Here's how it works: Google will create a custom From address for you based on an additional email account you are using to send mail from. In order to comply with established Internet email send protocols, Google also provides in the email header information your "real" or "main" email account as well as the second account you are using.

Sound confusing? It is. Stick with me.

If I send an email to you from my gaydbook.com account and you're using Outlook, the From line in Outlook will read a little something like this:

david@bolesuniversity.com on behalf of david@gaydbook.com

Ick and Ew!

It's ugly. It's awful. It isn't Google's fault. Google includes both email addresses in the full message headers for your email to prevent abuse. If Google didn't include both addresses for the Internet mail relays when they speak to each other, some nefarious people would use that lack of sender verification to spam others.

So Google does the right thing and makes everything upfront and clear to the mail servers. It can look funny to a recipient, however, and that's why you should beware of the possible perils of "The Curse of the On Behalf Of Curse."

Take some solace in knowing most email clients, however, are smart enough to parse the right email address you intended from the message headers and then just provide your From address using the single address you intended.

Label Works

You're almost finished with this chapter, but there are a few features I want to share with you before you wrap up here. Certain features just help you work better and smarter.

Let's work with labels! If you haven't been using labels to help sort your mail, now is the time to start kicking it! In your email settings, click on Labels to bring up that interface, as illustrated in Figure 4.41.

The labels you choose to create here are up to you. I prefer to have a few labels. I created one called GAYD for "Google Apps for Your Domain" that I started a year ago.

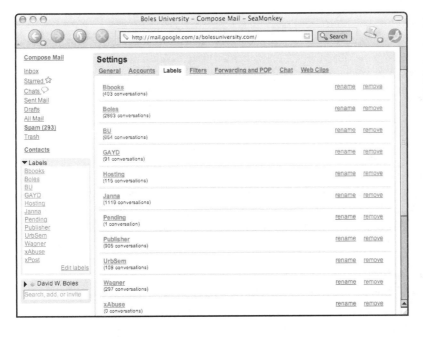

Figure 4.41
Pick a label, any label, as long as it makes sense to you. That's the only thing that matters.

> **Note**
>
> In helping you manage your email, Google prefers to use labels instead of a traditional folders interface because, for now, in Google's view, all your mail is in one giant ocean. Folders are like a series of lakes that do not interact or flow into each other. There is no interrelationship between folders (just like there is no water flowing between lakes), which is why Google prefers to use labels, which can and do share information across each other. One email can have many labels instead of being in a single folder, and all your mail is in one ocean waiting for you to fish it out and then point to it with labels, filters, and other categorizations and relationships that you alone control and direct.

Using Filters

Once you create some labels, you can really get fancy and begin to create some filters that will order your email into findable niches. You don't need labels to use filters, but while you're creating a filter to set up rules of interaction for your email, adding a label can help keep things keen in your mind. Filters are highly customizable, and I create a lot of filters every day to ratchet down my important and pending messages. I also use filters to rid myself of any spam that the Google spam filter misses.

> **Caution**
>
> The most important thing to remember about filters is that you can make them incredibly specific or entirely general, depending on your needs. I find that using too much specificity can cause problems in message recognition. It seems to me that a couple of criteria flags are enough of a separation from the ocean of messages I get a day to get the important stuff effectively sorted. The main caveat you must always remember is that if you make a filter too strict it won't be invoked much at all.

Filtering on a New Domain

In Figure 4.42, I want to create a new filter based on the criteria of my new email address: david@gaydbook.com. When I'm ready to move on, I'll click the Next Step button to continue the customization process. You can view some of my previously created filters at the bottom of the screen.

Applying the Label

The next step in creating a filter is to choose the right label. You can create a new label on-the-fly by choosing the last option (New Label) in the pull-down option menu, as shown in Figure 4.43. I will use my previously created GAYD label to indicate mail sent to my david@gaydbook.com email account. When I'm done I'll click the Continue button; the new filter will be taken live!

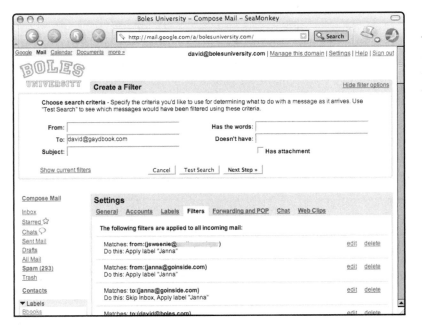

Figure 4.42
The first step in creating a Google Apps mail filter is to create the criteria by which you want the filter to abide.

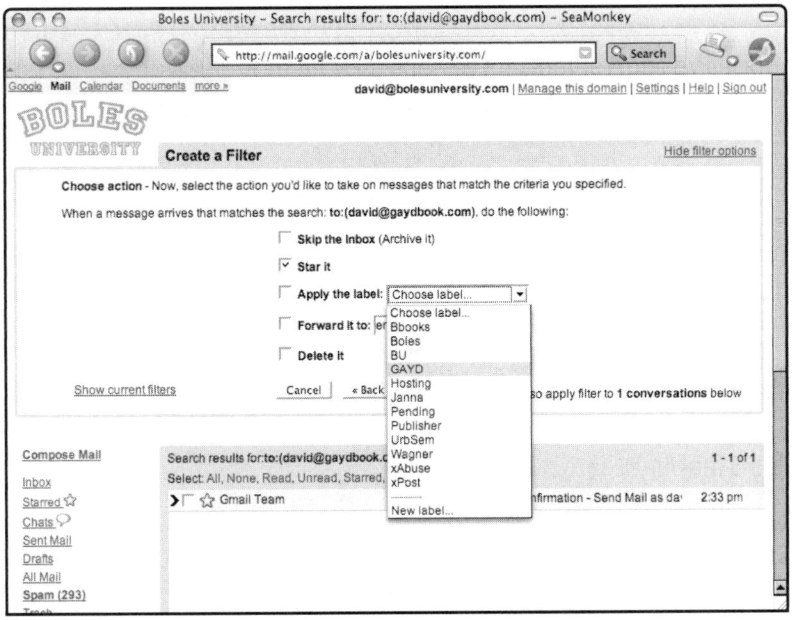

Figure 4.43
Pick a label, any label, or create one of your own!

Forwarding and POP

Another feature you can set up in your settings is pushing your Google Apps Gmail via forwarding to another email address or pulling it from a regular, standalone, email client. Using POP, you can choose to keep a copy of your mail in the inbox. You can archive the copy or you can delete it, as Figure 4.44 demonstrates.

> **Tip**
>
> When I POP my Google Apps Gmail from my iPhone, I prefer to keep all my Boles University email in my inbox in case something goes wonky between Gmail and my iPhone and the messages are munged or lost.

Figure 4.44

Here's how to forward and/or POP your Google Apps Gmail.

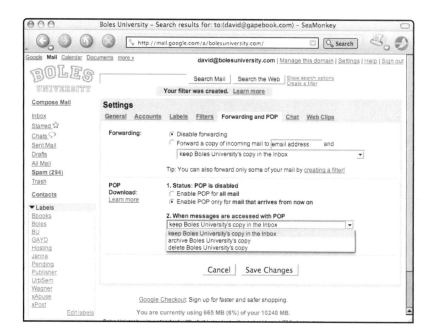

Clip That Web with RSS Feeds!

Finally, and in conclusion for this mega-chapter, if you click on Web Clips while you're in your Google Apps Gmail settings, you will find a wonderful feature that, when enabled, will let you see RSS headline feeds in your mail application. Figure 4.45 shows you the interface, and Google Apps provides a plethora of default news and headline sources. You can even search for your favorite feed by entering a topic or URL in the search box.

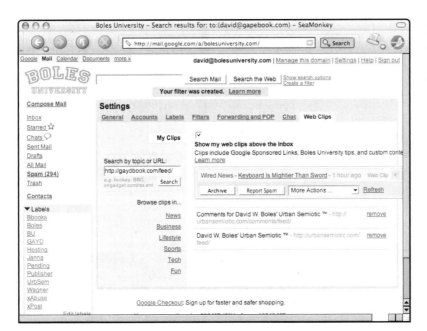

Figure 4.45
Customize your Web clips
here and add new content
to your Google Apps Gmail
interface.

Note

I prefer to delete all the default Web clips and add my own RSS feed from my blogs. This gives me a particular personalization that I find pleasing, and it's a great way to determine whether your blog comments and posts feed are updating throughout the day.

Figure 4.46 shows the position and reckoning of the RSS Web clips from my blog concerning an article I wrote on the iPhone. Every time you load an email or refresh the page, you will get a new Web clip to fire.

Figure 4.46
You can see the Web clip dynamically update with every browser refresh.

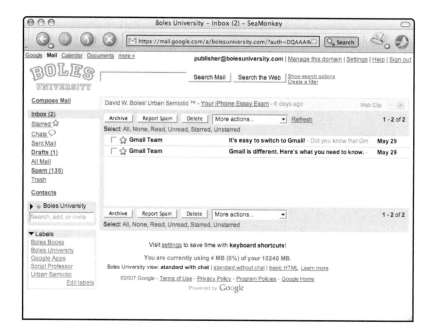

Coming Up Next

In this chapter, you learned how to add new users, manage existing users, and best set up the backend of your mail service via your Google Apps Dashboard to reflect the security and convenience settings that most appease your workflow. Then you worked with your domain alias email addresses and did some extra work on accounts verification. Then you parlayed some filters and labels and Web clips to your administrative advantage. In the next chapter, you'll put your Google Apps Calendar to work for you. You'll customize the Calendar so all your users are on the same page and in touch with each other's goals and timetables!

5 Scheduling Your Domain Calendar

In this chapter, you will set up the ability to share information and schedule objects via the Google Apps Calendar. You'll also allocate resources, learn how to manage multiple calendars, and find the best method for inviting and meeting the demands of your day using the Google Apps Calendar interface.

A Calendar for All Seasons

Figure 5.1 shows you the personalized login screen for the Calendar application. You can see that you are given a fine welcome by the Google Apps system and three nuggets of informational text. You can get an overview of your projects, you can easily share information, and you can always be aware of your calendar events even if you are not online. You can also see that my beautiful URL (http://calendar.bolesuniversity.com) has become the long and ugly URL (https://www.google.com/calendar/hosted/bolesuniversity.com/render), as discussed in Chapter 4. One of the first things you'll learn to do is beautify your login URL with a sub-domain via your Google Apps Dashboard.

Setting Up Your Calendar

The first thing you need to do to get your Google Calendar rolling is log in to your Google Apps Dashboard. As you can see in Figure 5.2, click on the Calendar link in the lower-right area of the screen to begin. I am showing you the familiar Dashboard interface again. Notice that the Service Graph and user count are loading today in the middle of the page. Remember, sometimes that graph is there, and sometimes it is not. Google loves to change and tweak small things all the time, so what you see here might not be what you see on your screen.

Figure 5.1
This is the login screen for
your Google Apps
Calendar.

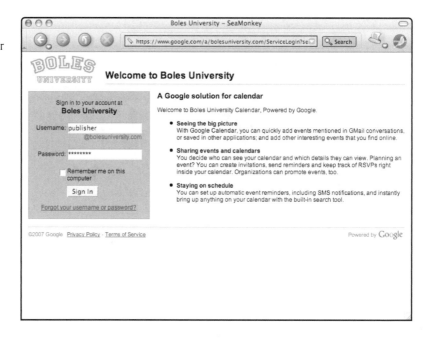

Figure 5.2
Click on the Calendar link
in your Google Apps
Dashboard to begin the
customization process.

Choosing Your Position

Click on the Calendar link in your Google Apps Dashboard to get to the Calendar Settings area, as shown in Figure 5.3. The first option allows you to choose your position on the Internet by creating a sub-domain when you click on the Change URL link. You can use "calendar," or "cal," or plain old "c" as your sub-domain, or something else you think will be easy for you and your users to remember. The process for creating a sub-domain is the same as the mail domain process you set up in Chapter 4, so I won't go into those hard details again here. I will, however, remind you once again of one friendly caution.

Caution

If you add a custom sub-domain to your account (and the domain was not registered through Google), you must—MUST!—create a proper DNS zone file CNAME entry for that domain. Otherwise, you will not be able to use the sub-domain to use your calendar.

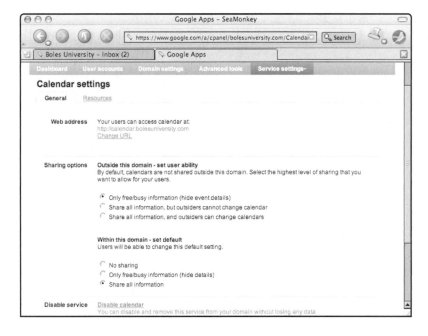

Figure 5.3

This is the General Settings view for your Calendar applet.

To Share or Not to Share

Another option for your consideration in the General Calendar Settings is the option to share your calendar. I prefer not to share calendars outside my domain because I have sensitive information, and I don't want my business or the business of my people being published on the Internet via a public Web site address.

You can choose how much or how little information you want to share beyond your domain. Interdomain sharing is also a setting you can manipulate. Sometimes you don't want your own users sharing calendars if you are doing private, internal work. I choose to share all information because we are all working on the same goals within the domain.

Outta Here!

You do not have to offer a calendar at all if you are concerned about people creating calendars and tracking the wrong things. Click on the Disable Calendar link to remove the calendar from your Google Apps Domain setup. You can always re-enable your calendar later if you miss your seasons.

Creating and Managing Resources

If you have Google Apps Premier or Education Edition, you can create and manage resources, as indicated in Figure 5.4. Resources are neat things because you can spread them out across your domain but keep complete control over them in a single interface. Click on the Create a New Resource link to add another resource. You can also delete a resource you don't use any longer by clicking the checkbox and choosing the Delete Resource(s) button.

> **Tip**
> *Resources* doesn't just refer to conference rooms and things that are found in conference rooms. A resource could be an intern, a car service, or a racquetball court. Anything you own or operate can be reserved for use by making it a Google Apps Calendar resource.

Next, you are presented with a series of text boxes you need to fill in to create your new resource, as seen in Figure 5.5. You're only required to name the resource. I'm calling my new resource Video Projector. You don't have to create a type or a description unless you have several varieties of a resource. Then you might want to be specific so people know which video projector you intend to reserve. When you're finished, click on the Create Resource button to return to the main Resources view.

I created a couple of new resources—a rehearsal hall and the video projector—as you can see in Figure 5.6. The Resource Successfully Created indicator above my Dashboard menu bar is confirmation of my accomplishment. In this view, you can also see the type of resource and its description. You can reorder that list of resources by clicking on the column heading. You'll soon learn how to reserve these new resources as you begin to work directly in the Google Apps Calendar for your domain.

Figure 5.4
You can create and share Calendar resources for use across your domain.

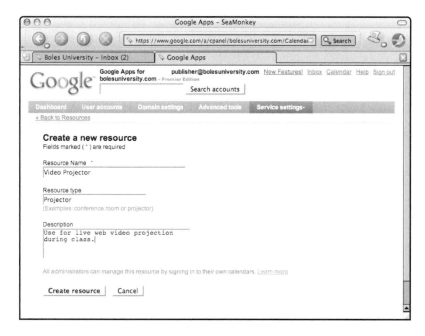

Figure 5.5
Name and then create the resources you intend to share.

Figure 5.6

Here is the list of my recently created Calendar resources.

Google Hates You and Your Little Calendars, Too!

My hope is Google will not hate you as much as it hates me when it comes to the Calendar. Of all the Google Apps services, I find the Calendar to be the most problematic, rude, discourteous, and frankly, mean. The Calendar hates me.

HATES ME!

At least once a day, I get throttled by calendar timeouts and flickering "saving" messages and dead server stops.

They frustrate me.

Maybe I have too many calendars? Perhaps I change my schedule too much? I might drag-and-drop appointments too often between too many days?

I don't know what the problem is, but I get a lot of timeouts, server errors, and refusals from the Google servers when loading my Google Calendar.

When Google Apps begins to act up with my Calendar, I've learned to slow down. If that still gives the Google server fits, I just stop what I'm doing for a few minutes so what I'm doing locally can be properly replicated "there" in the Google server cloud.

If you experience similar wonkiness with the Google Apps Calendar, don't sweat it. Just take a break and try again later. That should give Google a good chance to get everything resynched on their end.

The Calendar Proper

Now it's time to log in to your calendar! In Figure 5.7, you can see the calendars for one of my Boles University accounts. The Boles University branded logo appears in the upper-left corner, so I know I'm in the right account and not a generic Gmail-associated calendar. The next thing you need to do is add another calendar!

Note

I prefer the Month view because I can see the big picture of my day, week, and month in a single glance. Day views are too limited and don't show a grand enough scheme of my things.

Figure 5.7

Log in to the calendar for your domain to begin customizing your settings.

Adding to Your Day

Google Apps creates a default calendar for you, but to really take advantage of your new, innate scheduling power, you need to refocus and realize the power of creating lots of different calendars to serve all the righteous aspects of your life. You can create a calendar for each employee that you can then use to track progress and assign tasks, and if you choose to share that calendar with your employee or staff, you can give certain privileges to allow changes to be made to the calendar.

You can also create project calendars, "to-do" calendars, calendars for your kids and friends, and even calendars that reflect your private thoughts and goals.

Creating the Calendar

You're now ready to create a new calendar. Click in the lower-left area of your Calendar interface and choose the down arrow near My Calendars, as demonstrated in Figure 5.8. You can create a new calendar or add a public calendar that everyone can read on the Internet. You can also add a friend's calendar if you know the URL your friend is using, you can subscribe to any public calendar using a URL, and you can import a calendar from another scheduling program like iCal or some other calendaring service. Click on Create a New Calendar to take the next step.

> **Tip**
> Untimed appointments in your calendar appear as big bars of color in each day, whereas timed appointments are colorized text and are staked to specific times of the day.

Figure 5.8
Adding new calendars is easy as a button click.

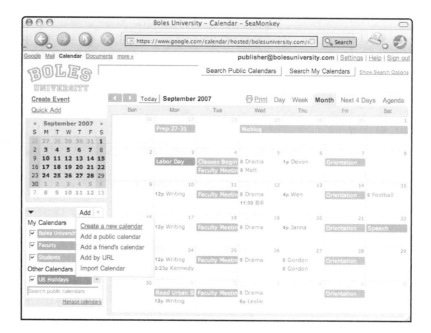

Those Devilish Details

Now, as you can see in Figure 5.9, you are located in the top half of the Calendar Details area for your latest calendar creation. You need to name your calendar. You can also provide a description and set a location and time zone. I prefer to keep the names of my calendars short so that I can see the full title in a single line in my main Calendar view. If you title your calendar with too long a name, your space will be taken up by two or three lines and look junky and unfinished. "Boles University" is a better calendar name than "David W. Boles University."

Figure 5.9
Name your calendar in this screen.

Two Can Share in This Game

Figure 5.10 indicates the bottom half of the Calendar Details area, where you can choose your sharing options with the Internet and your sharing options within your domain. I prefer to not share anything unless it is with a specific person. You can also set the control you want to give someone over the calendar you've created. The choices are these:

* *Make changes and manage sharing:* This option gives total control over how your calendar appears to another user. Your calendar will appear in their My Calendars area instead of the generic Other Calendars section. People with this level of sharing can even prevent you from controlling your own calendar, so use this option with care. This Sharing option is good for co-owners, spouses, and blood relatives you actually like.

* *Make changes to events:* This Sharing option allows someone to add and delete events but not delete you as a calendar owner/manager. This setting is good for people you really trust, such as agents, assistants, and managers.

* *See all event details:* This option makes the specifics of your details known. No changes can be made by anyone sharing this calendar. This setting is good for co-workers and company associates inside or outside your domain.

*   *See free/busy information (no details):* This Sharing setting is the most genetic and least lethal of all. Viewers can see when you're busy and free but not where you are at what time and what you're doing there. This setting is good if you must publish your schedule on the Internet or some other place where you cannot control all the viewing eyes.

When you've made your decisions about sharing, click the Create Calendar button to save your new calendar and its settings.

Caution

Remember that this calendar-sharing business strikes both ways! You might have a lot of calendars to which you subscribe where you can see only free/busy information (no details), which might hurt your powerful pride a bit. Wouldn't it be fun to know which person under a single Google Apps domain made the most changes and manage sharing access to other people's Google Calendars? I think we just created a new gold standard on which to base the idea of a real power broker!

Figure 5.10

Decide your public-, private-, and people-specific calendar-sharing options here.

Associating Appearances: Creating Custom Color Categorizations

The four C's of using the Google Apps Calendar is to always remember the power of color with this titled mantra: create, color, custom, categorizations.

Google Apps Calendar lets you categorize your calendars by color, and you have a lot of colors to use. Do not take the color application lightly that Google creates by default, and on its own volition, for you.

You be in charge of picking your true colors! There is power in associating appearances by clicking on the down arrow next to each calendar. You can pick colors in the same family, say, bright green, green, dark green, and have three calendars that are interrelated in title and color!

You can also choose to have all the "bright" colors represent urgent events, while "muted" colors are the drab doings of each day.

Remember that color is your friend and your invisible associate. Use color to your advantage. Google offers you these color picks for a reason, so realize your full potential and start creating color!

Clicking and Dragging

Figure 5.11 demonstrates that the new research calendar I just created is alive and well and living with the other My Calendars in the left sidebar. When you want to create a new appointment, you can click-and-drag it to the calendar. In the Day view, you can click on 8am and then drag your mouse down to 12pm. When you release your mouse click, you will immediately get a balloon asking you to fill in the details of the appointment. You can click on the down arrow in the Which Calendar window to choose the calendar assignment that best describes your new task. When you're done, click Create Event, and your appointment will be saved.

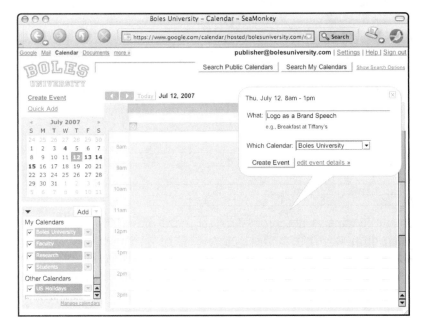

Figure 5.11
Click-and-drag to create a new appointment.

Popping In

In the Month view of your calendar, you can also pop-add an event by clicking anywhere in the window of the day you want to choose, as indicated in Figure 5.12. You fill in the What text box, pick your calendar from the drop-down menu, and then click on Create Event when you're satisfied.

> **Note**
>
> Your Google Calendar is smart enough to sort of read your mind. If you enter "Google Scholar 2-5pm" in your appointment window, Google will know you want the appointment to run from 2 to 5pm. That saves you both steps and time because you don't have to edit your event for specifics after creation.

Figure 5.12

Click anywhere on a calendar day to quickly add an event.

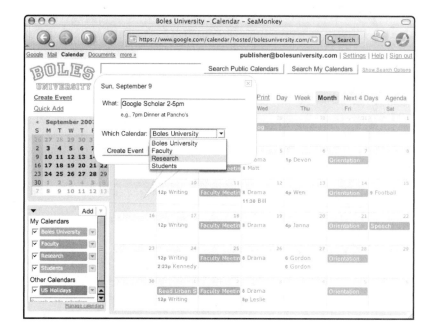

Public Calendars

Google has culled some great calendars together for you. Choose the Add a Public Calendar option from the My Calendars drop-down menu to see a snapshot of available calendars, as shown in Figure 5.13. When you see a topic that interests you, just click on the Add to Calendar button. All the information captured in that calendar will appear in the Other Calendars section of your main Calendar view.

Beware the Loser Sports Calendars!

I especially like adding sports calendars to my Google Calendars. I currently track the Yankees, the Mets, and the Huskers via Calendars. I can turn the views on and off for each calendar by unchecking the checkbox next to each calendar name in the main view.

Beware that not all of these public calendars are winners. I've gone through at least five different "Yankees" public calendars because a really good public calendar offers more than just a schedule. The final Yankees calendar I settled upon was one that also added the scores and the win/loss record of the Yankees.

Now that's special because most calendars are only forward thinking: "the games of whence to come." My Yankees calendar, however, loves history and it is updated—backdated, if you will—by its anonymous calendar operator to include the scores and win/loss records after the Yankees play each game. That's a neat feature because you can easily page back through the months and get a fine snapshot of where and how the Yankees are performing in history. This year, you might want to forget every single game they've played. Let's hope 2008 is a better Yankees year.

Figure 5.13
Google makes adding public calendars easy. Just make sure you pick the right one if several on the same theme are available.

Making All Calendars Jump Through One Hoop

You have learned how to set the features for individual calendars. Now it's time to head into your Calendar Settings so you can set up some general settings that will universally be applied

123

to all the calendars you own or subscribe to via Other Calendars. You get there by clicking the Settings link in the upper-right corner of the main Google Calendars view.

This Is How You View It, View It

As Figure 5.14 demonstrates, you are now in the upper-half view of your general Calendar Settings. You can choose a plethora of options here, from your preferred language and country and time zone to your date and time formats. You can even show weekends and add a custom view.

> **Note**
>
> I like my weeks to start on Sunday—I'm old school, I guess—and I prefer my default view to be the Month instead of the Week view. My wife loves the Day view, probably because her days are filled with meetings and are time based, whereas my days are more project based. She needs the minutiae of her day revealed, and I need to see the big picture—how days become monthly deadlines.

Figure 5.14
Customize your calendar with default views and format indices.

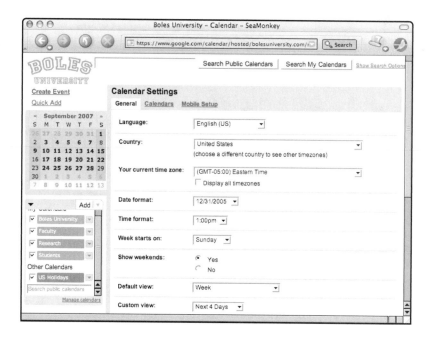

The lower area of the general settings is shown in Figure 5.15 and holds many important personalization gems. You can set your ZIP code location, choose to show the weather (always show your weather; it's informative and stays out of your way!), decide if you want to see the domain events you have declined, and decide if you want invitations automatically added to your calendar. I like to see declined events, and I also enjoy having invitations auto-added–that method makes everything clear and serves as a great reminder when you wonder back on events and invitations that came before. A Change Password link is also provided to help concentrate your security. When you have all the options you want in place, click on the Save button and you're done!

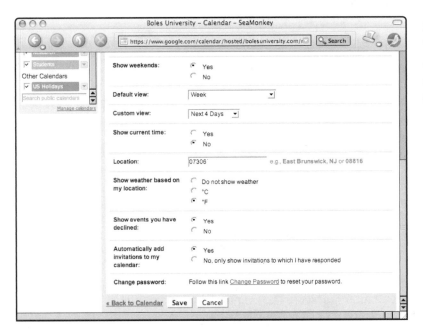

Figure 5.15
You can have your Google Apps Calendar show declined events and auto-add invitations.

Check, Please!

Now let's reserve a resource that you previously set up in the Google Apps Dashboard.

1. The first thing you need to do is head into the main Calendar view.

2. Click on a day to create a new event.

3. Click on the Edit Event Details link in the appointment balloon that pops up.

4. In the main event view, click on the Check Guest and Resource Availability link under the Days selection.

5. Figure 5.16 shows the Find a Time reservation window that will dynamically expand to fill your screen. Here you can check your attendees, add people, reserve resources, and click-and-drag the appointment time. When you're done setting the details, click the OK button to return to the event details screen.

Figure 5.16
You can find a time to reserve your resources here.

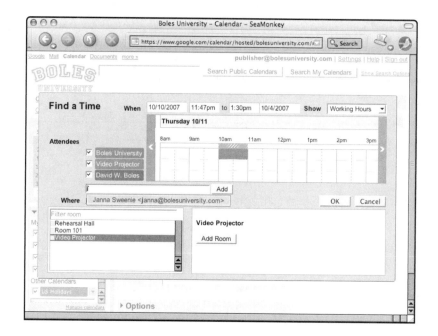

6. Now you're taken back to the upper half of your event details screen, as shown in Figure 5.17. The information you entered in the previous pop-up box is now in place. The location, which calendar, and the description are all modifiable here if you want to add even more detail or invite more guests to the event.

7. Finally, scroll down the screen to see the lower half of your event details, as depicted in Figure 5.18. You can give yourself a pop-up reminder for the event, and you can reset the privacy options.

8. When you're satisfied, remember to click the Save button. If you make changes without saving and just click the Back to Calendar link, you will lose all the modifications you made.

Caution

Your privacy choices are Default, Private, and Public. They are based on your personal calendar settings. If you have all of your Google Apps Domain Calendars set in your Dashboard as private and not shared beyond your domain, your calendars will remain private even if an individual user chooses to set his or her calendar as public.

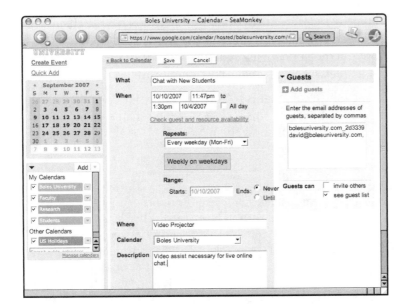

Figure 5.17
The previous pop-up box automatically fills in your event detail resources.

Figure 5.18
You can mini-manage your Calendar (even the privacy settings) here if your domain administrator has provided public options for Calendar sharing.

Play Hide and Show

If you have a lot of calendars, you can quickly get overwhelmed with too much information as your schedule gets packed. You have two ways of cleaning up your Calendar view, as you can see in Figure 5.19.

The first is to simply turn off your calendar by unchecking the checkbox next to the list of calendars in the left sidebar. Unchecking a calendar prevents the information connected to that calendar from displaying in your main Calendar view. You might want to turn off all your calendars except for one to get a precise view of what's happening with a single calendar.

The second way of hiding and showing a calendar is by heading into your Calendar Settings again and choosing the Calendars option. From this screen, you can rename your calendars, directly choose to share them, and also hide or show them.

> **Note**
>
> When you hide a calendar, you are not removing the information; you are removing it from view in your list of calendars in the left sidebar. You will most likely hide calendars that don't change a lot but that you want to follow. For example, I have a "Google Doodles" calendar I love because it shows the Google logo modifications for holidays and special events. I also hide "Phases of the Moon," "Weather," and "Holidays" because that information is static, not created by me, and I can't manipulate it, so why show it and clog up my sidebar? I still want the information, and the calendar information still appears there, but making it visible in my sidebar is unnecessary. You can always unhide a calendar by going into Calendars Settings and clicking on Show.

Figure 5.19

You can hide and show any calendar from this interface.

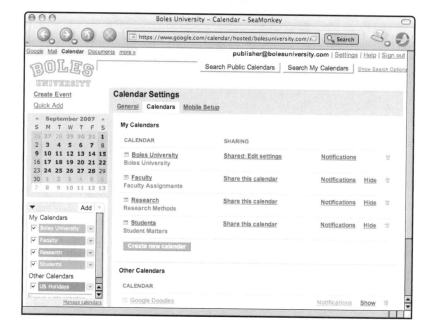

Going Mobile

One of the greatest things about your Google Apps Calendar is you can take it anywhere you like because it goes mobile on your cell phone or PDA! You can communicate with your Google Apps Calendar from afar, and it can touch you at various times throughout the day.

The first thing you need to do is to tell your calendar where and how to find you. You do that by entering your cellular number in the Mobile Setup section of the Calendar Settings area, as demonstrated in Figure 5.20.

> **Tip**
> You can visit your Google Apps Calendar online with your cellular phone or PDA by typing in your calendar's address. My address is http://calendar.bolesuniversity.com, and you will need to log in and then interact to see that your calendar is in a specialized, really tiny view! You can even do quick add appointments, view the previous day's agenda and the next day's agenda, in addition to your default current-day view.

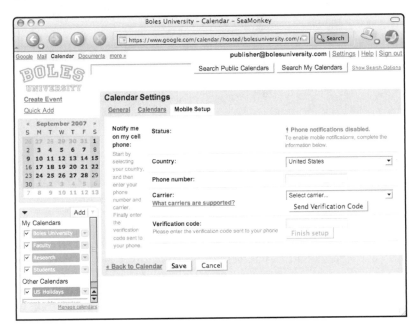

Figure 5.20
Enter your cellular phone number to begin your Google Apps Calendar mobile setup!

Next you need to choose your cellular phone carrier. As you can see in Figure 5.21, the list of phone carriers Google supports is quite large and specific. After you choose your carrier, the calendar will send a text message to your phone or PDA. You need to enter that special string of numbers in the Verification Code box. When you have verified that text string, click on the Save button; your phone will be set up for mobile alerts!

> **Caution**
> If you have a lot of calendar alerts set for send notification to your phone and don't have an unlimited text plan on your cellular phone account, beware that you might be charged by your cellular provider per text or SMS message.

Figure 5.21
You must choose your cellular phone carrier for your mobile setup to continue.

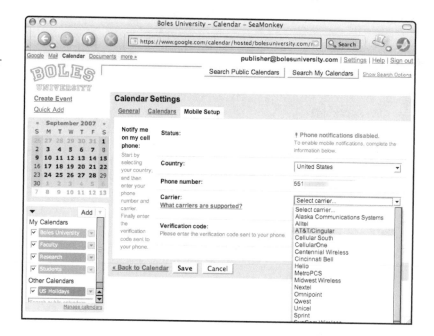

Never Pick Your Nose, But Do Choose Your Alerts!

You have three options if you want to get an alert from a Google Apps Calendar. Click on any calendar to get the detail view in Calendar Settings and choose Notifications. From that screen, as shown in Figure 5.22, you can be alerted to any event via an email message, an SMS/text alert sent to your phone, or a pop-up screen on your computer as you work. You can choose the notification to alert you anywhere from five minutes before the event to as long as a week before.

You can also decide how you want to be alerted. You can get new/changed/cancelled invitations as you wish and also have a daily agenda zoomed to your phone to keep you in your own Google Apps Calendars loop.

Note

Notifications are set up per calendar. There is no universal setting for calendar event notifications. You must choose to set notifications for every individual calendar you use.

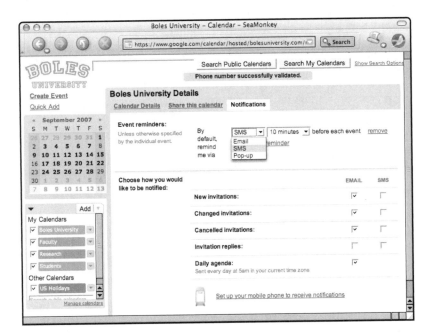

Figure 5.22
Make your mobile notifications active on this Calendar screen.

Push Me, Pull Me with SMS and Your Google Calendar

Did you know if you send a text message to "GOOGL" and include search terms you will get a text message back from Google Search with the very first search return? That's pretty neat because the power of Google Search is in the tips of your fingers!

You also have a similar ability to interactively push and pull information from your Google Calendar to your mobile phone. Here's how you do it.

Send a text message to "GVENT" (48368) with the details of your event, say, "Dinner Janna 8pm Saturday." The event will be auto-added to your default Google Apps Calendar. This method works like the quick-add feature.

You will get a text message returned from your Google Apps Calendar confirming the successful addition of the event to your calendar.

You can also text the word "day" to "GVENT," and your Google Apps Calendar will zing you back a text reply with all your events for the day.

You can text the word "next" to "GVENT" to have your next scheduled event sent back to you from Google Apps Calendar via text.

Texting "nday" to "GVENT" will result in a return of tomorrow's schedules events, as held in your Google Apps Calendar!

Beware if you have multiple calendars–including those that might be on the regular Google Calendar system–that GVENT works only with the calendar you last used to set up your phone. If you are using GVENT and getting back wrong appointments or a message that your phone is not registered, reset your phone with your Google Apps Calendar to force the right calendars to connect with your mobile phone.

Once you set up SMS, you will get notifications for all events across all calendars associated with your Google Apps Calendars.

GVENT currently works with the following cellular carriers: Alltel, AT&T, Cellular One, Cincinnati Bell, Cingular, Dobson Communications, Nextel, Qwest, Sprint, T-Mobile, US Cellular, Verizon, and Virgin, and the list is always expanding. You can visit the expanding list online:

http://google.com/support/a/users/bin/answer.py?answer=43409&topic=11681

Share and Share Alike or Never Share Once

Let me show you a few other angles on how to share a Google Apps Calendar. Figure 5.23 shows I am presently sharing my Research calendar with Janna Sweenie. I can set her access level right there and save it–she'll get an email notification on any changes I make–or I can click on the tiny trash can icon and remove her entirely from accessing my calendar. Make sure you click on the Save button to ignite any changes you made.

From one of my Boles University accounts I will choose to share my Research calendar with another one of my Boles University accounts. Figure 5.24 demonstrates the sort of email that's sent to the other party as notification of the initiated share. These calendar shares are automatically added to the intended's calendar.

When you then load your calendar after a new calendar has been shared with you, Google Apps determines the default color of the shared calendar, as indicated in Figure 5.25. Notice Boles University in the Other Calendars view in the left sidebar? That is my new calendar. Notice in the main Month view, the Weblog string of events and the Classes Begin notification were added to my calendar.

Tip

If I could manage and change the Sharing settings of the added calendar, it would appear under My Calendars instead of under Other Calendars. My Calendars shows only those calendars that I distinctly own and operate.

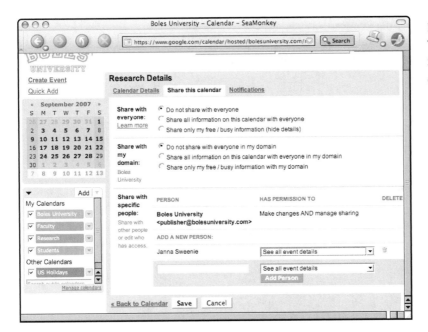

Figure 5.23
You can change calendar
Sharing access levels or
delete shared users.

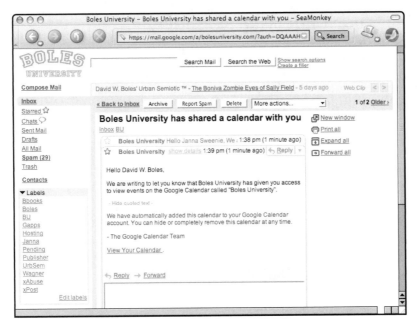

Figure 5.24
This is the email notifica-
tion for a shared Google
Apps Calendar.

Figure 5.25

Google Apps Calendar added the Boles University calendar to my view.

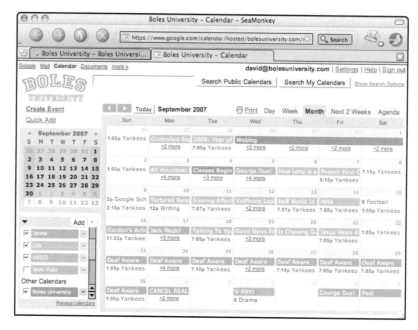

A Privacy Warning: Your Underwear Is Showing!

I want to show you a visual example that should serve as a warning to you when it comes to unwittingly sharing a calendar. Shield your eyes as you sneak a peek at Figure 5.26. I performed a simple Google search by entering my last name into the Search Public Calendars option in the Calendar interface. You can see what looks like rather personal and perhaps even confidential calendar information right there, in full view, for the world to see and wonder upon. (Those results have nothing to do with me. Those results are other people out there who share my last name and who are providing their personal bits for online consumption.)

I call this sort of unfortunate schedule sharing "showing your underwear" in public!

I have given their names a bit of a box blur to try to shield their identity a little and to protect them some from their own public stupidity, but that information is still, as of this writing, right there, out in the open and entirely public.

Don't think that if you don't explicitly give out the Web address of your public calendar that your calendar can't be found in public. It can. Everything public on the Internet will eventually be found and indexed and put into a search engine somewhere. You're seeing the proof of the pudding.

I don't think that sort of information should be visible for the world to see, and just think, if someone less honorable than us had some sort of weird, bad intentions, they could quite easily, and surreptitiously, follow those folks by simply adding the public calendar to their Other Calendars and then sort of virtually stalk them by getting to know their routines and habits.

Scary, huh?

Pull up your pants and pull down your skirt! There are bad people in the world; giving them a free peek at your underwear only encourages them to dig into you deeper.

Consider yourself warned!

Figure 5.26
Beware of the consequences of making any calendar public on the Web! You are searchable and easy to find!

To Do or Not to Do?

One of the biggest features missing from Google Apps Calendar is any sort of integrated to-do list as of this writing. I say "as of this writing" because I hope that by the time you read this, some sort of Google-supplied to-do feature will be added to the Google Apps suite.

In the meantime, if you want to create a shifty sort of workaround to-do using the Google Apps Calendar, create one calendar called To-Do and another calendar called Complete.

Go into your Calendar Settings and hide the Complete calendar.

Add your untimed appointments for the day to the To-Do calendar. When you finish each task, edit the appointment and change the calendar assignment from To-Do to Complete; your To-Do is to-done!

It's clunky, but it works.

You can also just delete the tasks you add to your To-Do calendar via appointments if you wish, but moving them to a hidden Complete calendar saves your achieved tasks for future reference. You can see them again by choosing to show your Complete calendar in the Settings area.

How to Invite and Accept Calendar Events

Now I'll quickly show you how to invite and accept Calendar events using two Boles University accounts of mine—David and Publisher. If you're on either end of the event you'll know what to do or how to respond.

Eagerly Inviting as Publisher

First, as evidenced in Figure 5.27, I click on November 3 in my Calendar view to create an event in my Publisher account for a discussion concerning antisocial networking, and then I click on the Edit Event Details link to invite myself to my own meeting.

Figure 5.27

You can test the invitation and acceptance feature of your Google Apps Calendar if you have access to separate user accounts.

As you can see in Figure 5.28, I'm still in my Publisher account, and I have invited myself on my David account to my own meeting. When I'm done filling out the details, I click on the Save button at the bottom of that page–that you can't currently see–to put the event on my other account's calendar.

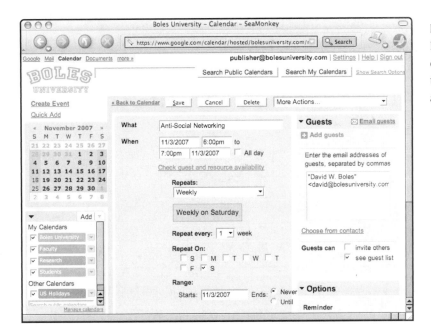

Unabashedly Accepting as David

Time to switch hats! Er, accounts! Now I'm in my David Google Apps Calendar, shown in Figure 5.29. Do you see the antisocial networking reservation bar for 6pm along with a giant question mark (?) in the event itself? If you click on the question mark, information about the invitation will pop up, and you can choose to accept the invitation, decline it, play coy and say "maybe," or just delete the dang thing outta your sight forever. You can also make the event longer or shorter. You'll be prompted by your calendar to save the changes or restore to the original circumstance.

Your Daily Agenda

Before I wrap up this chapter, I want to show you in Figure 5.30 what a Daily Agenda email looks like from the Google Apps Calendar when it hits your box around 5am each day. I really enjoy the color-coding of the event, which matches the color I chose for the calendar.

Don't confuse an Agenda email with a Reminder email from your Google Apps Calendar. Reminders look entirely different, and they're coming up next!

Figure 5.29
Clicking on a calendar invitation with a question mark will provide choices for attending or not.

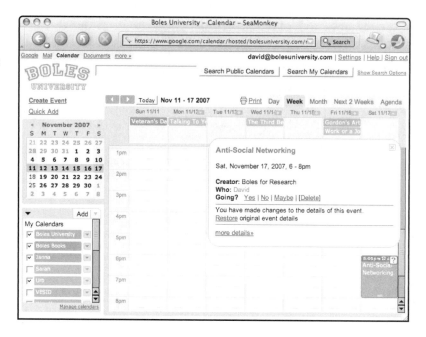

Figure 5.30
This is the Daily Agenda that Google Apps Calendar will email to you every morning at 5am if you choose to enable that notification.

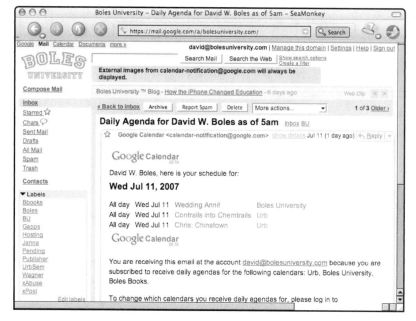

A Friendly Reminder

I couldn't finish the chapter without giving you a quick shot of what a Google Apps Calendar Reminder email looks like, compared to a Daily Agenda. You can take a gander at a Reminder in Figure 5.31. The design of the Reminder email is innovative and inspired, and frankly, quite lovely to read with the whole "envelope as semiotic meme" applied, enforced, and unfolded.

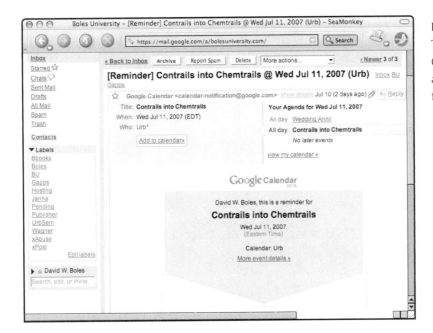

Figure 5.31

This is a Google Apps Calendar Reminder email and should not be confused with a Daily Agenda.

Always Remember and Never Forget

Congratulations! You are now an expert in every way when it comes to forging your schedule—and the calendars of others—in setting up and mandating how you want Google Apps Calendar to serve you. In this chapter, you set up your calendar sub-domain and compared the merits and dangers of private and public calendars. You set up events, reminders, and invitations and color coded them all to make a life on the Web with form, context, and style.

6 Building Your Domain Web Pages

In this chapter, you'll use Google Apps to create some Web pages. I am not a tremendous fan of how Google Apps provides and manages Web pages. They just kind of point to their Google Pages service without adding any extreme special coolness you might expect from Google. If you're an experienced Webmaster, you likely won't have much use for Google Apps Web Pages, but if you're fresh and new to creating Web sites, you will have a delightfully easy time getting your ideas online.

Setting Up Your Pages

Google calls the ability to create a Web presence "Web Pages" in the Google Apps Control Panel. Note that the link in the bottom-left corner of the Control Panel Dashboard (shown in Figure 6.1) is not called a Web site. Google is sort of publicly winking at you because they know they are really only offering you the ability to create a few Web pages right now.

Caution
Perhaps in the future Google will find a way to enhance the service with more power and features. You really don't want to run a sophisticated Web site using Google Apps Web Pages. Right now you don't even have FTP access. All file uploads are done one at a time via a Choose File browser window.

Working with the Service

Figure 6.2 shows you the meager offerings for getting your Web Pages settings operational. You can go directly into editing your pages on the Google Page Creator Web site, you can create a sub-domain entry, or you can turn the service on or off. Let's click on the Change URL link in the Web Address area to poke around there a bit.

Figure 6.1
Set up your Google Apps
Web Pages by clicking on
the link in the lower-left
side of the screen.

> **Tip**
> If you decide to activate Google Apps Web Pages, you can always disable the service later without losing any files or settings.

Figure 6.2
The Web Pages Settings
screen in the Google Apps
Control Panel provides few
settings you can modify.

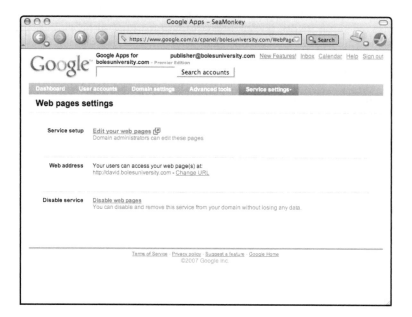

Return of the CNAME Thang!

If you want to personalize your Web pages with a sub-domain, you have to return to the CNAME monster, as demonstrated in Figure 6.3. You can use the default long URL for your Web pages if you like, but if you want to create your own sub-domain, you need to change the DNS zone file record for your domain by adding the appropriate entries with your domain registrar.

Before you move along to actually managing, editing, and creating your Web pages with Google Apps, I want to show you a shortcut for modifying all the sub-domains on a single page. If you click on the Change URLs for All Domain Services link, you can personalize every one via a single page.

Note

Make sure you know the CNAME you plan to use. For detailed instructions on setting your CNAME entry, please refer to Chapter 3.

Figure 6.3
Create a sub-domain for your Google Apps Web Pages and click on the Continue button when you're ready to save your changes.

One Stop Change All

Note in Figure 6.4 that you have now entered the Change URLs for Multiple Services page! This feature is sort of hidden–probably because it provides great power in a single effort, which the Google Apps inexperienced might mess up. This page gives you one quick and ingenious way to modify all the custom URLs for your Google Apps experience. You can also slam back to the default URLs here.

Tip

Remember, if you add or modify any sub-domain, you need to save the information on this page and then modify your DNS zone file accordingly to reflect the CNAME changes and additions.

Figure 6.4
On this single page, you can modify all the custom sub-domains for all your Google Apps services.

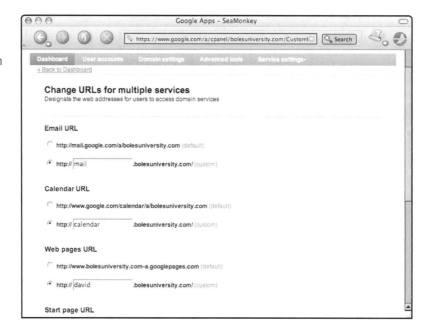

To Host or Not to Host?

You can be creative with your Web Pages sub-domain naming. I chose "david" to provide my whole name in the URL as david.bolesuniversity.com, and I use that URL to demonstrate the features of Google Apps Web Pages even though I host most of the Boles University Web on my own private server.

I decided to use and exploit the Google Apps Web Pages sub-domain for my domain. It adds some functional depth and an emergency URL in case my Boles University Web site becomes unavailable for reasons beyond my control.

david.bolesuniversity.com and bolesuniversity.com are hosted on different servers, so I am guaranteed that, in the case of an unforeseen calamity, at least one of my hosted sites will be live.

I could host all of bolesuniversity.com on Google Apps Web Pages, but I don't like the design and management limitations, and I am especially wary of the unknown bandwidth limit cutoff–more on that later in this chapter. I am struck that I have 10 gigs of storage for my email, but only a meager

100MB of server space for my Google Apps Web Pages Web site, and you can't currently use a favorite icon or a ROBOTS.TXT file.

I could host all of Boles University on Google Apps Web Pages without needing a separate server, though. If your Web site needs are simple and not severe, that might be a good way to have a Web site with easy maintenance.

So, I split the baby. I have a "david" link on my Boles University Web site, which links back to Boles University from my bolesuniversity.com presence. I like and appreciate the redundancy.

Making the Page

Using the link on your Control Panel for Web Page Settings, click on the Edit Your Web Pages link. You will then be taken to the Google Page Creator login screen, as indicated in Figure 6.5. Be sure to enjoy the informational mini-promo for the service in bullet-point form.

Note

Don't be confused by the naming convention Google uses for its established service and the Google Apps version of the same feature. Google Apps Web Pages is Google Page Creator, but not the other way around, because those who use the free Google Page Creator feature don't have access to Google Apps Web Pages unless they have a domain registered with the service.

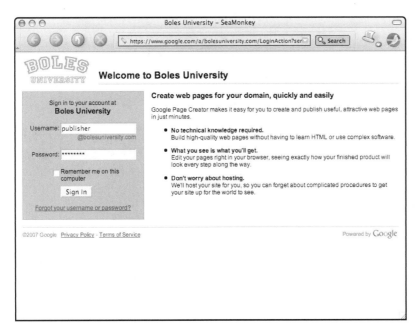

Figure 6.5

Log in to your Google Apps Web Pages service by heading into the Google Page Creator feature.

Evidence of Bad Behavior

Okay, now I'm going to show you some evidence of my bad behavior in that I haven't been regularly checking in with Google Apps Web Pages to see what is new and updated. In Figure 6.6, I am not taken to my Google Page Creator as I expect. I am instead taken to an interesting welcome page that looks remotely familiar from the first time I set up the service a year ago! I've never actually seen this page before, I guess, and when I click on the link in the upper-right screen that reads I'm Ready to Create My Pages, I am taken to a link at the bottom of the page:

Figure 6.6

This is an advertisement for Google Pages and not the management screen I expected.

Figure 6.7 shows me a Terms and Conditions screen, and I have to check a box agreeing to be let into the Google Page Creator site. Hmm! I find this strange, since I've had my Boles University pages on the site for well over a year. Obviously something has changed since I last logged in, and as I told you, I don't use the Page Creator much because it is not terribly powerful. The lesson I am learning in sharing the evidence of my bad behavior with you is that you should regularly log in to all your Google Apps services—even if you are not making any modifications or changes—to note any new contract terms. I had no idea Google Apps Web Pages/Google Page Creator made this change until I logged in with you to write this chapter. Click on the I'm Ready to Create My Pages button to continue.

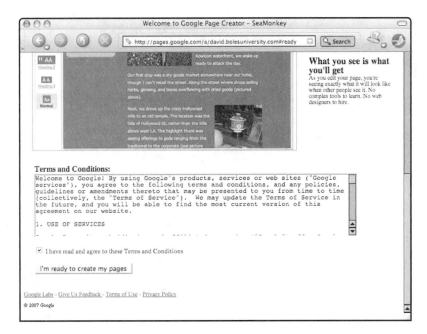

Figure 6.7
You must agree to
Google's terms and
conditions before you
can create your Google
Apps Web Pages.

Editing a Page

Okay! Now this looks better! Figure 6.8 shows the Edit Page view for my main homepage on
david.bolesuniversity.com. You can drag-and-drop elements from one action box to another. If
you want to view your page as others will see it on the Web, you can click the View Live link.
You can also use the Unpublish link at the bottom of the screen to remove your page from
public view. Let's use the View Live link near the top of the page.

Note

If you make a mistake while editing or want to revert to previous changes, you can always use the Undo
button to reverse the current state of your edit. The Redo button can help you perform repetitive tasks.

Looking Live

Figure 6.9 shows you the live view of the page you were just editing. You can see that the edit
buttons on the left side and the dotted lines indicating the action boxes have disappeared. The
ultimate hint that you are live and not in edit mode is the URL in the browser window: http://
david.bolesuniversity.com is a real, live, established Web site.

Figure 6.8

Here's how I edit the homepage for david.bolesuniversity.com.

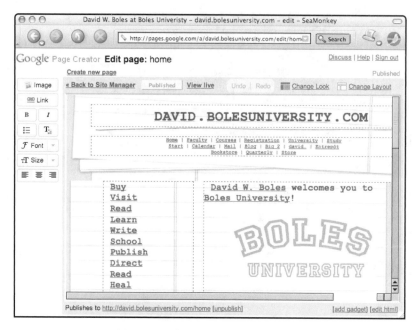

Figure 6.9

Here's the live public view of david.bolesuniversity.com.

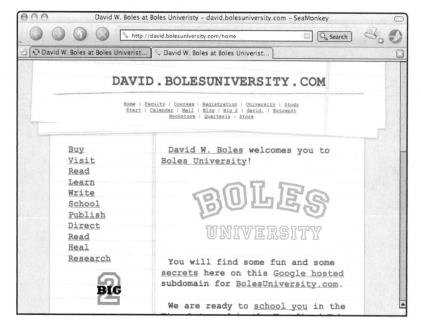

Pick a Look, Any Look

After looking at that ugly yellow paper I'm using as a background element for my site, I've decided it's no longer working for me. It is too loud, too obnoxious, and sort of high-schoolish for such a luxe university–but it was also my only real "school" choice available in a template when I first created the page. So I need to head back into the Edit Page view and choose the Change Look link near the top of the page on the right side to see if there are any new looks available.

In Figure 6.10, I have scrolled down to the bottom of the Choose Look page, and there, highlighted on the left side, is my current look, called Paper Legal Pad. The Paper Plain White look next to my current look looks good, so I'm going to click on the icon to load that look into my page editor.

Tip

Changing the look of your pages modifies the fonts, background colors, and images. Your content will remain untouched after the change.

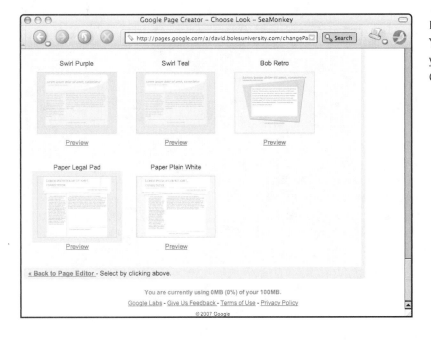

Figure 6.10
You can change the look of your Web pages on the Choose Look options page.

Pretty in Paper

Oh, wow! The Paper Plain White look looks pretty good. I like the look and feel of this elegant university-like theme. I'm keeping it! To make this look live, I have to click the Publish button. That will save my file and also take it live for public view. Next, I want to view the options for the page layout. To the right of my Change Look link sits a Change Layout link that I will click next.

Figure 6.11
This is the Paper Plain White look in the Page Editor view.

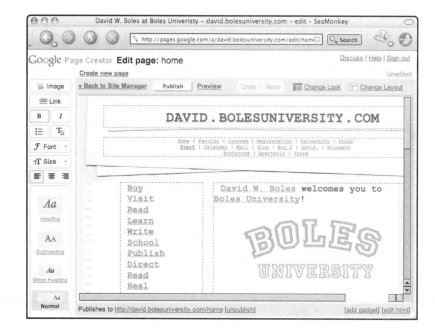

Modding the Layout

Now I have the option to choose the layout, as indicated in Figure 6.12. None of these options look any better than the layout I already have. I'm changing nothing! I click on the Back to Page Editor link at the top of the page to return whence I came. Any layout changes you make are reversible, and none of your content is modified when you play around with different layouts. Experiment to your heart's desire!

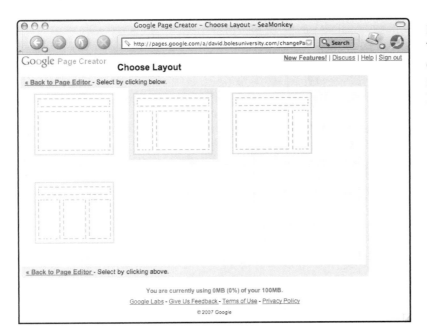

Managing Your Site

Welcome to the Site Manager, shown in Figure 6.13. You can find this main brain for your Google Apps Web Pages any time by clicking on the Back to the Site Manager link residing on any Editor page. From this page, you can modify all aspects of your Web site that Google Apps allows you to control. Clicking on a page icon will take you to that page in your Editor view. You can upload files. The page icon with the house on it represents your current homepage. Let's check out the Site Settings link residing in the upper-right corner of your screen to see where that takes you.

> **Caution**
> Always keep your eye peeled on the familiar usage thermometer at the bottom of the page if you plan to create and upload a lot of Web pages. That interactive thermometer will tell you how much of the 100MB of server space your Web site is currently using as well as how much space remains.

Setting the Site

Your Settings area, as demonstrated in Figure 6.14, gives you detailed information about your Google Apps Web site. You can change the Title tag on your pages here by filling in the Site Name text box. You are shown the URL that Google Apps Web Pages is currently pointing to, and

Figure 6.13

The Site Manager is the brain stem of your Google Apps Web Pages creation process.

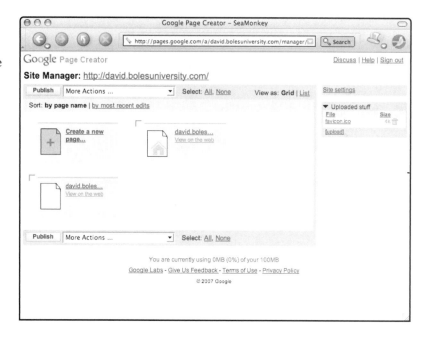

you can decide if you want Google to optimize the size of your images to make them load faster on the Web.

I also see there's a giant button asking if you want to enable experimental features. I'm pretty certain I already told Google I wanted all new and experimental features available here in the Web Pages/Page Creator setup, but perhaps that information was lost when I didn't log in routinely enough for their system. You can also tell Google you are hosting adult content—that will place you in an online quarantine where only appropriate eyes will be able to find you. Finally, you can just create private Web pages where no one but you and those you choose to tell can find your pages on the Web. Let's click on the Enable Experimental Features button and see what happens.

> **Note**
>
> If you want to change the URL of your Web site, you cannot do that here in the Settings page for Web Pages/Page Creator. You must go back into your Google Apps Control Panel and change the URL there.

Too Scared to Continue, but Too Curious Not To

Now I've done it! Figure 6.15 shows the giant warning screen from Google that loaded after I clicked my desire to enable the experimental features. How many people other than us bother

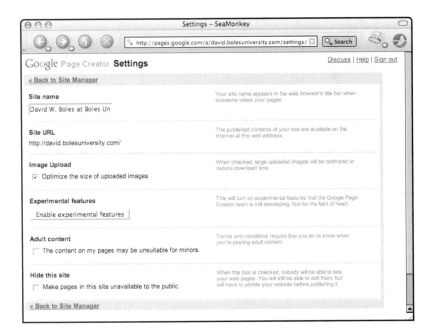

Figure 6.14
This is where you can invoke settings for your Web pages.

to read that huge disclaimer and just click the Yes button in spite of the Google humor daring you to click No? I'm a yes man, so I'm enabling the features, and I'm waiting for my site to blow up.

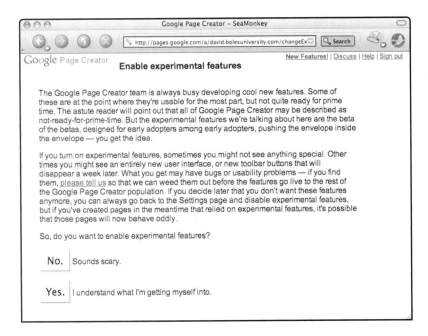

Figure 6.15
Do you dare to enable experimental features?

Searching for the Experimental

Okay, now I'm dying of curiosity to see what destruction I may have done to my site by enabling the experimental features. I return to my Site Manager, as seen in Figure 6.16. I don't see anything that looks new or scary or remotely interesting. Checking the More Actions drop-down menu doesn't reveal any particular suggestion of fun, although I did laugh out loud at the option to tell your friends about your new Web page! Google thinks of everything–and they'll even type the message for you. I think I'll click on the Create a New Page option and see if I can find anything newish there.

Figure 6.16

Nothing new or experimental here yet, so I'll keep clicking to search.

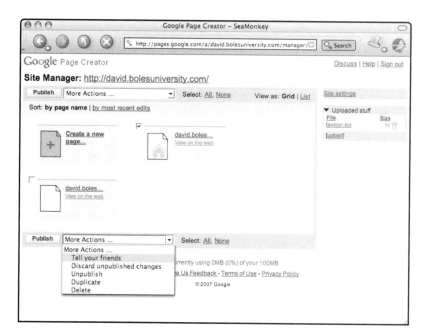

Secrets Found!

Ah-HA! I see in Figure 6.17 that my toolbar has moved from the left side of my screen and positioned itself along the top of my new page! If that's a new experimental feature, I'll eat my hat. It's hardly scary, but I think having the edit and formatting buttons on the top instead of the side is more user friendly. That doesn't mean the toolbar will stay there, though. Google loves to turn things around just when you're getting used to them–that's their nature and their company culture–and so that is also the necessary part of the delight of working with Google. They're always changing and thinking ahead. I'll type in a headline for this new page—Google Apps Administrator Guide—which also happens to be the title of this book!

Caution

You can see the headline I set for the page also became the name of the page. googleappsadministratorguide is nothing if not long and ugly. Beware of your default page-naming conventions!

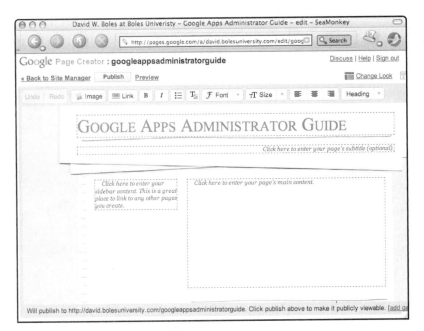

Figure 6.17
Voila! The edit buttons are now at the top of the experimental editing screen.

Link It, and They Will Come

Staying on the same experimental page you just created—as you can witness in Figure 6.18—I added a link to Boles University in the left sidebar. When you click on the Link button at the top of the page, an Edit Link window pops up at you. Using that pop-up box, you can link to a page you created, a file you uploaded, another Web address, or an email address. I'm doing a straight link to my own Web site, so I enter the URL in the text box and click on the OK button to create the link.

Adding Images

Web pages live for images, and I added one on the experimental page by clicking on the Image button in the toolbar. As seen in Figure 6.19, Google Web Pages/Page Creator offers an option to create different sizes of images to help make it best fit the page. I also linked the headline of this page, and I created some text to wrap around the logo image.

Figure 6.18
Creating links is as easy as filling in a text box.

Figure 6.19
Adding images to a page is easy and automatic.

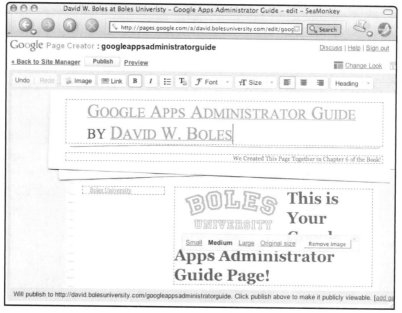

Tip

When you add an image, Google asks you to tell it the location of the image. I always have Google add the image from a live URL on the Internet because adding it as a file upload to Web Pages/Page Creator sometimes doesn't work. I've never had a file failure when loading my images from an offsite Web page I manage and own.

Spot Check

When you're in the midst of editing, it is always wise to spot check the status of your designed page outside the Edit view. Click on the Preview link to have the page load live, as you can see in Figure 6.20. I've added a few more links to round out the universal look of all my pages. Remember, you know you're live by looking at the URL in your Web browser's address window.

Note

Can you believe the name of the experimental page we just created is actually:

http://david.bolesuniversity.com/googleappsadministratorguide

Golly! That URL is just so long and ugly, I'll have to keep it so you can enjoy it live on the Web while reading this book!

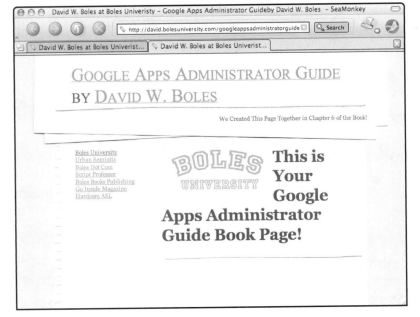

Figure 6.20
Preview your edited pages often to get a clear public view of what you're really creating.

Back to the Future Manager

Scooting back to the Site Manager in Figure 6.21, you can tell I've made a change in how that page is viewed. We're in List mode now instead of Grid mode–this isn't an experimental change–and you can get much more information in this fuller view of what's going on with your files. You can see the experimental page I created has a warning that says "in revision," and that means the page has been changed in the editor but has not been saved–or published on the Internet. You can also see a larger warning about the unsaved status of your pending page on the right side of your screen. Google is good at warning you about changes not being live.

Figure 6.21

Pages you edit but do not save are specially marked by Google to let you know the status of your live publications.

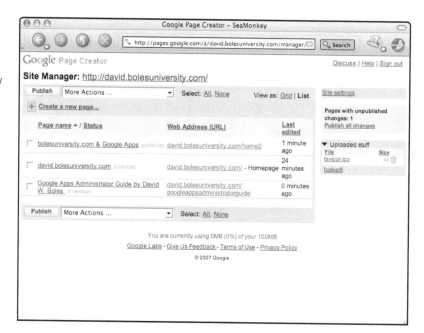

Gadget or Gewgaw? The Inquisition

Google is in love with gadgets. Gadgets are informational doodads like RSS feeds, games, weather indicators, and other information that has been compartmentalized into a drag-and-drop feature you can add to your Web pages to provide greater value to your service. I confess I am not big on these sorts of gadget gewgaws, but they do help quickly build content on a page. Here's how to find a gadget and insert one.

At the bottom of every page you edit, you will find an Add Gadget link in the lower-right corner of your screen. Clicking on that link pops up the main Google Gadgets page, where you can search all the gadgets. Simply click on those that interest you in order to add them to your page, as demonstrated in Figure 6.22.

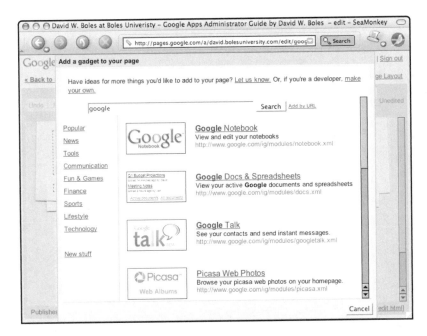

Figure 6.22
Google makes adding content easy via pre-programmed informational and functional gadgets.

Gadget Insertion

In Figure 6.23, I have added the Google Talk gadget. I can drag-and-drop that gadget anywhere on the page. The gadget will try to find its own space and fill a proper empty niche, so if your gadget is too big to fit, just keep working with it on the page by dragging it around with your mouse until it settles down.

Tip
You can drop a Google gadget only in a text box that exists. You can't drop a gadget into an undefined space. I had to insert some blank lines after my Apps Administrator Guide Book page to tell my Google Talk gadget it was okay to try to jam in there without damaging the rest of my design.

Gadget Inspection

Okay, the Google Talk gadget has been inserted, and it looks good in the page editor, but does it work and look good live on the Internet? It's time to force another live preview by publishing the page to the Web and viewing it as everyone else in the world would. Figure 6.24 confirms the Talk gadget loads fine, looks good, and does actually add an immediate sense of page-design sophistication to what was a rather ordinary experimental Web page.

Figure 6.23
The Google Talk gadget
has been added to the
Web page.

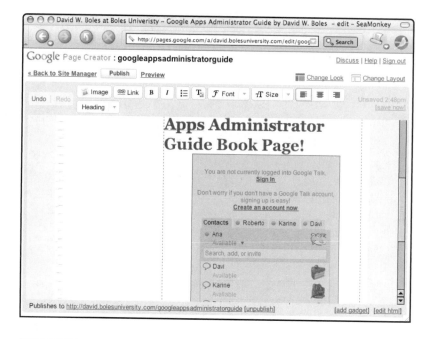

Figure 6.24
This is the Google Talk
gadget added to the
Web page.

Don't Ask, Don't Tell: Automatic Sitemaps and RSS Feeds

Not many people are aware that Google Apps Web Pages and Google Page Creator automatically create and then publish on the Internet a sitemap of every single file you have uploaded to your site—even if those files are not in public view.

DO NOT UPLOAD PRIVATE INFORMATION TO YOUR SITE!

My sitemap is located at http://david.bolesuniversity.com/sitemap.xml. Just replace my domain name with yours, and you can view your sitemap if you have uploaded any files. You can see my "favorite Icon" file is listed even though Google does not support that browser URL address image on its service.

I repeat my warning to you: Be certain you do not upload any personal information you do not want automatically indexed on the Internet because Google uses sitemaps to quickly index entire sites.

You should also be warned that Google automatically creates an RSS feed of your Google Apps Web Pages and Google Page Creator Web site.

My RSS feed is located at http://david.bolesuniversity.com/rss.xml. Switch your domain for mine. That means anyone can subscribe to your Web site content with any RSS reader at any time.

Before I Close, but Staying Live...

Before I wrap up this chapter on Google Apps Web Pages/Page Creator, I want to show you a live shot of the Boles University Web site I created and manage on my own server.

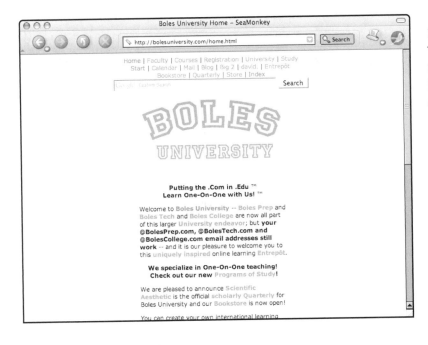

Figure 6.25

This is part of the Boles University Web site that I host and manage on my own private server.

Figure 6.25 brings you the clean design of that page, and it has a different look than the "david" Web page version hosted on Google Apps. I have complete control over the design of my self-hosted Web pages, and I can manage my disk space and bandwidth at will, which is important to keep in mind when you make a decision about hosting your Web pages with Google Apps.

Eating Your Bandwidth

The reason I host the main part of Boles University's Web site on my own servers is not only because of the measly 100MB of file space Google Apps offers for Web sites, but also because of the horrible possibility of creating a popular Web site and having Google cut you off without notice.

If you have too many visitors, your Web site will use up too much bandwidth, and the server will get overloaded from serving up so many pages. In practice, that's a dream come true! You have a popular Web site! People want you!

The risk you run with Google Apps hosting your Web site is that, if you become too popular, Google will turn off your site until you have fewer visitors. That's a conundrum—when is too many visitors too many? When Google tells you so. Except Google doesn't directly tell you. Google will not say how much bandwidth use is too much, and their official statement on the matter from their Web site reads like this:

> "Exceeded bandwidth limit" basically refers to how much traffic your site can get during a given time. While we do have a limit set on it, we are not at liberty to disclose the amount at this time. If you exceed the bandwidth limit on your site, please know that your site will come back as soon as your site's traffic has fallen below our set amount. Please keep in mind that Google Page Creator is still in Labs, and we are continuing to look for ways to improve the service and appreciate your feedback.

You can keep your eye on this wacky Google non-policy policy by following this link on your own time:

http://www.google.com/support/pages/bin/answer.py?hl=fr&answer=60424

If you don't find that cloudy warning frightening enough, take a look at Figure 6.26, which I found on a Web site hosted by Google Pages—I blurred the name to protect the innocent. As I understand it, Google Pages and Google Apps Web Pages run on the same system with the same warnings and limitations. If that's true, visitors might come to your site and find this statement instead of your content.

Chilling.

Figure 6.26
Here is the fateful "over-the-bandwidth" error your visitors might encounter if your Google Apps Web Pages become too popular.

Managing, Editing, and Surfing Around

In this chapter, you worked on getting your Google Apps Web Pages set up in the Control Panel for your domain. You also added some interactive features to your Web pages while learning how to edit and save pages for public consumption. In the next chapter, you'll learn how to set up a specialized start page that Google Apps offers to all users of your domain as a special shared starting point.

7 Crafting Your Domain Start Page

In this chapter, you'll make a universal start page for all the users of your domain. This start page can serve as a common touchstone for all your domain tasks and communicative interaction. You'll also learn how to set up the Google Apps Start Page features in your Control Panel.

I will say up front that of all the Google Apps, the Start Page is one of the most confounding features for me. It is the only "feature" that is not listed as "beta" in your Control Panel Dashboard, yet it doesn't quite work right, seems incredibly immature in function and design, and is more confusing than enlightening.

This chapter is consequently filled with lots of caveats and warnings—but that is only to help you make the best use of the most crippled Google app until it can be fixed for maximum functionality. My hope is those changes will be implemented by the time your hands touch this book.

What You See on the Start Page

If you head over to http://start.bolesuniversity.com, you will see something like Figure 7.1, which anyone on the Web can view. This page is public, and the information is clickable even for visitors who are not members of your domain. Be sure you don't include any proprietary or private information on your start page unless you want to share it with the world!

Unfortunately, http://start.bolesuniversity.com is only a placeholder URL. The instant you enter that Web site address, you are redirected to the Google version of the page located at http://partnerpage.google.com/bolesuniversity.com

That long URL is neither pretty nor easy to remember, but there isn't anything you can do about it right now.

Figure 7.1

This is the public Google Apps Start Page. Anyone can see it on the Web.

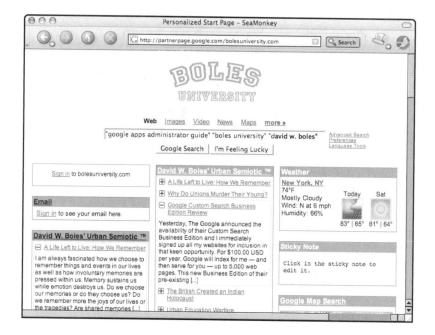

Getting Around the Start Page's Poor Construction

There is a strange lack of default vital content for creating your Google Apps Start Page, such as embedded links to your entire sub-domain redirects for Mail, Calendar, and Docs. The fact that those default links are missing is puzzling.

To get around this start page construction default, you can do what I did and create a semi-start page of your own using Google Apps Web Pages or by using your own server and HTML page.

If you head over to http://bolesuniversity.com, you will see a landing page for all my domains. In the upper-left side of the screen, you'll see a link for Boles University that will take you to that homepage.

In the Boles University area, I have created quick links to my Google Apps login pages–via Secure HTTPS as we discussed in Chapter 4. These links are for my domain users and include Mail, Calendar, Docs, and even the start page proper!

This need to do a login workaround for vital services seems to be a strange missing feature of the Google Apps Start Page. My workaround may be a little clunky and perhaps even unattractive, but it gets the job done quickly, and my users don't have to wade through and wander around on a start page with no precreated links to basic services.

Start Me Up!

When you click on the Sign In link on the public start page, you are taken to the login screen shown in Figure 7.2. I enjoy showing you these default login pages because they are full of information that Google thinks is important. In this instance, there isn't much here from Google that I haven't already covered or anticipated.

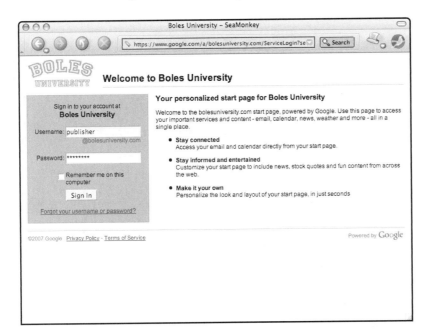

Figure 7.2
All Google Apps login pages hold fresh information that is of-the-moment.

What You Got

Now that you're logged in, as demonstrated in Figure 7.3, you can see that your email inbox and calendar have been added to your private, proprietary view. This is called the *personalized start page.* You can add modules and gadgets to this Google Apps Start Page as an administrator or as an end user, and we'll discuss those tasks more in-depth soon in this chapter. You can also see that the Boles University logo and custom color scheme are incorporated into this page. You'll work on those settings as well, but before I get to that, let me show you what a real start page should look like. The design and implementation are courtesy of your friends at Google.

Tip

You may also see the Manage This Domain link on the right side of your screen if you have the proper administration privileges. That link will take you directly to your Google Apps Control Panel.

Figure 7.3

When you log in to your start page, you can see your email and calendar.

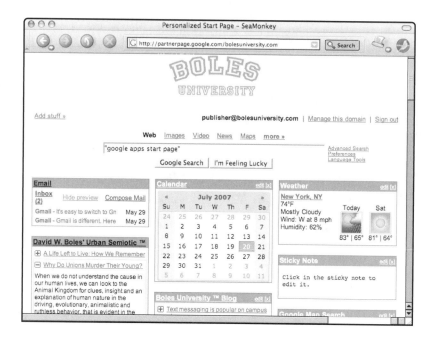

What You Should Get

When you look at the beauty ensconced in Figure 7.4, you see how cunningly wonderful Google can be with a start page if they so choose. What you are seeing in that image is not a Google Apps–created start page, but the general iGoogle start page that Google offers to anyone on the Internet. You can create your own iGoogle Start Page by heading over to: http://www.google.com/ig?hl=en.

You can easily modify your page to include features and functions that delight you. You can pick themes–currently cartoonish–and have your page dynamically change throughout the day to reflect the weather and/or the time of day. This start page is what you'd expect from a Google Apps Premier Edition setup, but it is not yet available to Google Apps users. I miss the easy beauty of the iGoogle design when working on my Google Apps Start Page. I've included this brief, but beautiful, diversion because this functionality must and shall be built into the Google Apps Start Page workspace setup. My hope is that his will be a reality by the time you read this chapter.

Setting Up the Start Me Up!

When you log in to your Google Apps Control Panel, the Dashboard provides with you a direct link to the setup of your start page, as indicated in Figure 7.5. I still find it wildly amusing that the "beta" label is not applied to the Start Page link found at the bottom of the page. The Google Apps Start Page is the most unfinished and fluid version of all the bundled Google Apps!

Figure 7.4
The iGoogle Start Page is what the Google Apps Start Page yearns to become.

Figure 7.5
Click on the Start Page link to construct your Google Apps Start Page features.

Note

You can access the area to edit your start page only from your Control Panel link. There is no outside URL you can currently use that will log you in directly to the Start Page editor. You must always enter through your Google Apps Control Panel to manage your start page settings.

Artfully Accessing the Editor

Entering the settings page, you will witness three rather meager customization choices artfully presented for your perusal. You can customize your start page, and you'll do that momentarily. You can create a sub-domain address—as ever, please see Chapter 3 for detailed instructions on how to take a new unique URL live in your Google Apps setup. Finally, you can turn on the service or remove the service from your Google Apps setup.

Note

You can also view the last time your start page was published live on the Web. You can use this page as a counter-correction against any changes you make in the Start Page editor to ensure the changes you make were recorded by the Google Apps system and actually become live for new users to come.

Figure 7.6
The Start Page Settings page is the start to customizing the start page.

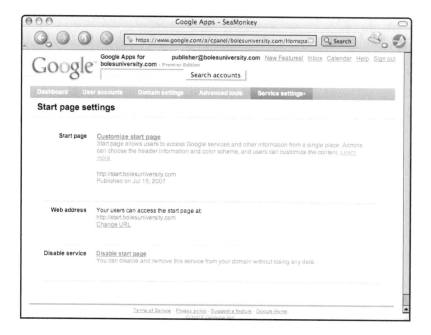

Starting the Start Page Editor

After clicking on the Customize Start Page link in your Control Panel, you are whooshed over to the official Start Page Editor page, as indicated in Figure 7.7. On the Get Started tab, you can modify and set up your Google Apps Start Page, and you can follow the steps on that page or take a fuller and deeper process of modification by following the links along the top of the page. You'll use the top links for this section of the chapter, because they will remain in place throughout the process and so can be used as signposts for continuation. Click on the Layout tab and let's get going!

Figure 7.7

You can begin to customize your start page with styles and content from this initial page.

Laying It Out and Locking It Down

You have two options for laying out your start page, as shown in Figure 7.8. In actuality, though, you only have one choice as the domain administrator: Locked Column. If you pick the Fully Customizable option, anything you set on the start page can be removed, changed, and messed up. You need some modicum of control over your content for announcements, RSS feeds, or any other feature you want everyone in your domain to have. That means your choice for layout must always be Locked Column. You can see those beautiful padlock icons in the first column of the three-column default Google Apps Start Page layout. Those padlocks mean anything you drag-and-drop there will remain there for all your users, in perpetuity, until you alone change the content.

Figure 7.8
Pick the Locked Column option to guarantee all users will see the same information in at least one column of your start page.

Your Colors Define You

Clicking on the Colors tab brings you to the top half of this delightful page demonstrated by Figure 7.9. You can choose the colors you want to use in designing your Google Apps Start Page. Because Boles University uses a darkish orangey color for our logo, I picked complementary colors like white, dark brown, light brown, and dark orange for my start page.

> **Caution**
>
> Picking colors is super easy. Almost too easy! If you click in the wrong area, you might unwittingly change a color you did not intend to change. Make sure your mouse pointer isn't in any active selection boxes when you design your colors, or you might just pick a look you did not consciously intend!

The bottom half of the Colors page, shown in Figure 7.10, contains the Preview Color area, where you can test the look and feel of your start page color picks. I'm using black and white text on a burnt orange background for headlines, a white background and light-brownish links, and darker-brownish visited links. Play around with your color choices—you might be surprised by making some unique color connections—and when you're ready to move on to the next step, click on the Header and Footer tab to continue.

Figure 7.9
Pick a color, any color, for
your start page design!

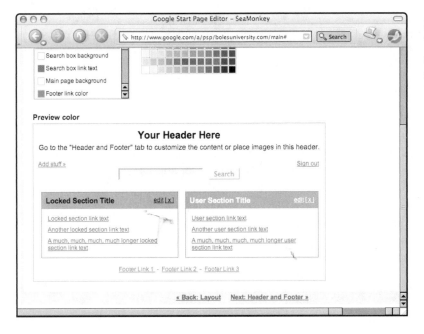

Figure 7.10
You can test your color
choices in this Preview
Color area.

Heading Over Heels

Now you've landed on the Header and Footer edit page, and although there may not be any "heels" here–other than your footer–to fall heads over, you can still do a lot of fun and precise customization here. Some things, as you will soon learn, are untouchable. Figure 7.11 show you the editing layout; doesn't it look familiar? It has the same interface and editor spirit and functionality of Google Apps Web Pages/Page Creator discussed in Chapter 6. You design and implement your header and footer here. A *header* usually consists of your logo and a brand phrase or other custom imprint. A *footer* usually holds links and other universal information you want to remain on every page, even if your end users add pages to your Google Apps Start Page. I prefer simplicity in my design, so my header is my Boles University logo, and my footer contains links to the Boles University homepage, Boles Stuff for sale, my Urban Semiotic blog, and the Boles University blog.

Notice when you click on the Google Privacy link in the footer, a blue warning box pops up and tells you that must keep that link as part of your Google Apps terms of service! Talk about linked, locked content! If you click the Edit HTML text link in your toolbar, you can directly fiddle around with the page's raw HTML.

> **Tip**
> Google requires you to keep the Google Privacy, Terms of Service, and Help links in your footer. You cannot change those links or the words that provide these links. Those links are owned by and belong to Google, and you have to work around them in your footer design.

Give It to Me Hard and Raw

You can see hard and raw HTML in Figure 7.12. Please don't mess around on this page by clicking on the Edit HTML link in Design view unless you understand that "hard and raw" has nothing to do with sex or passion and everything to do with the low-level and the hardcore power of how Web pages are parsed and loaded by servers and Web browsers on the Internet. Be careful using this Edit view; it takes some guts to risk messing up your page styles and the look and feel of your start page.

Next, let's move on to adding to the body of your page–the content between your header and your footer–by clicking on the Content link.

Figure 7.11
You can customize your header and footer from this editing panel.

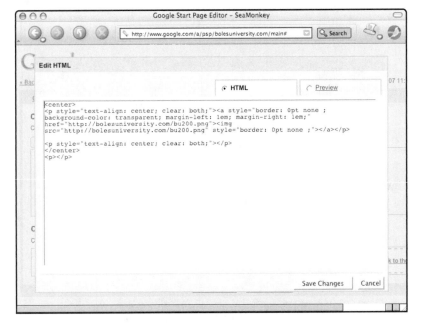

Figure 7.12
This is the hard, raw, HTML view of your custom header and footer page. Don't play here unless you know what you're doing.

Finding Meaning in Content

Now it's time to fill in the guts of your start page. As you can see in Figure 7.13, my start page is already filled with some proprietary stuff I added for my users, such as a link to email, the RSS feed to my blogs–all in the Locked Column portion of the page–as well as some obligatory links to some news sites and weather. You can see the content is loading live because my email inbox is showing the number of unread messages, and the News module is fresh as well. When you first stop here to set up your start page, Google will populate all your columns with some content. You can keep it or delete it at will. You can move content between columns by dragging-and-dropping gadget modules.

Figure 7.13

You can populate your start page columns with content and functional information.

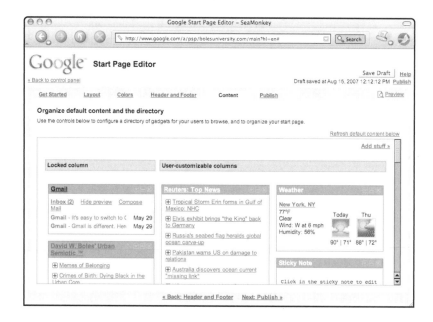

To remove content, click on the x in the upper-right corner of the module heading. You can add new content by clicking on the Add Stuff link found on the right side of your screen. Let's add some stuff!

> **Note**
>
> When you want to drag-and-drop a content module from one column to another, grab the headline portion of your gadget module with a held mouse click–but without touching the linked headline–and drag it to the new location. A successful module "grab" will result in the module becoming a dotted outline. It will fit in by moving other gadget modules out of the way as you test its new placement.

176

Building Content

Okay, when you click on the Add Stuff link, you are taken to your version of the screen you see in Figure 7.14. Because I have previously added special content–my RSS feeds from my blogs–Google assumes I want to modify or add to that special content. Even though the content is already added, Google for some reason allows me to create duplicates by clicking on the Add It Now button. You have three ways to add content. You can use the provided Search box to find content. You can directly add the URL of content gadgets–like an RSS feed–by clicking on the Add by URL link next to the Search Content button. Also, you can click on the links found in the left side of your screen under the Custom Sections heading. Let's click on the Google Apps link to see what's lurking for us there!

Figure 7.14
Adding content is as easy as clicking on the Add It Now button.

Embedding Meaning

After clicking on the Google Apps link, you are presented with three Google content choices to add (see Figure 7.15): Gmail, Google Talk, and Google Calendar. Let's have a little fun and click on the Add It Now button for Google Talk, just like you did in Chapter 6 when you added Google Talk functionality to the Google Apps Web Pages. Google Talk also is coming up in Chapter 8, so you're embedding meaning in the start page and this book by invoking the power of the past and the promise of the future! When you're finished adding content, click on the Back to Homepage link to see how the new content looks on your start page.

Tip

You can add more than one content gadget module at a time. Click on all the Add It Now buttons you like and then click on the Back to Homepage link for an overall view of your new content.

Figure 7.15
Click on the Add It Now button for Google Talk to add that module to your start page.

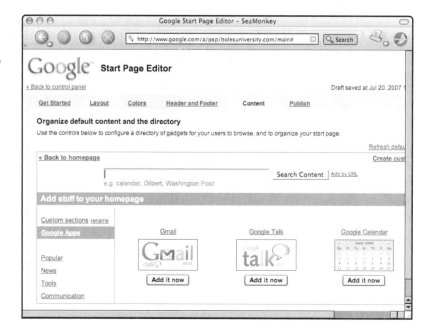

Checking New Content

Back on the Start Page Editor page (Content tab), you can see the Google Talk gadget now appears as the first choice in the middle column (see Figure 7.16). Remember that placement, because it will inexplicably move when you get the live view of the finalized content found on your Google Apps Start Page. When you're satisfied all your content is in the right place and looking good, move on to the final step. Click on the Publish tab found at the top of the page.

Figure 7.16
When you add new content, be sure to check the placement to make sure it appears as you wish on your start page.

Publishing Your Start Page

When you're ready to take your start page live, click on the Publish Updates button found on the Publish tab, as shown in Figure 7.17. On this page, you can see the full, long, ugly, direct URL to your start page. You will be provided an alert highlighted in yellow telling you the time and date of your successful start page update. You also have the ability to remove your start page from the Internet if you feel something went amiss and you need to start over. Note the warning on the page that reads "Changes made to the default content will only appear for new users." You can read more about that strange warning in the sidebar entitled "When Changed Content Doesn't Change," later in this chapter.

Caution
Remember, you cannot use a secure HTTPS URL to reach your Google Apps Start Page. The secure protocol will take you to a generic Google homepage instead of the one you designed with Google Apps.

Figure 7.17
Take your Google Apps Start Page live by clicking on the Publish Updates button.

Verifying Changes

Just because Google says it has published your start page changes doesn't mean it actually happened without a hitch. Be a wary consumer and head out live on the Internet to take a look at your Google Apps Start Page. Make sure you clear your browser cache first. Is everything there and cogent? Is your Locked Column content looking copasetic? Are you satisfied with your content gadgets? Looking at my saved start page in Figure 7.18, I am alarmed to find—without being logged in—that the Google Talk gadget appears at the bottom of the middle column and not at the top, as you saw in Design view. This is one of the unpredictable things with the current Google Apps Start Page editor. This setup appears to vary from domain to domain. Sometimes the content stays where you put it, and sometimes it just moves or entirely vanishes from sight. More on this strange phenomenon can be found in the sidebar entitled "When Changed Content Doesn't Change," later in this chapter.

Note

Do not sign in to your domain when you verify the changes to your Google Apps Start Page. Log out if you are logged in so you can see how the start page looks with the most recent saved customizations. Logging into your start page will not show you the changes you made.

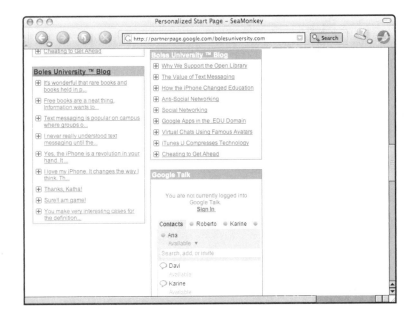

Figure 7.18
My Google Talk content gadget has mysteriously moved to the bottom of the middle column even though I placed it at the top of the column in Design view.

When Changed Content Doesn't Change

Making changes to the Google Apps Start Page can be confusing even for the most jaded designer and jaundiced Webmaster, because what you change is not always what you will get.

For some reason no one can really answer, changes currently made to your start page only appear for new users!

If you registered for your domain and then made a few fun changes to your start page just to test it out, those initial changes are what you will see. If you re-create your Google Apps Start Page from scratch, those changes will not be visible to your existing users. Google sort of warns you about this on the final Publish tab:

> "If you update your start page, changes made to the header, footer, colors, and locked columns will appear for new and existing users. Changes made to the default content will only appear for new users."

Isn't that strange?

As I write this, Google is being bombarded with requests by Google Apps administrators like you and me to change this no-update policy for the start page. I hope by the time you read this, you'll have some sort of Google-provided button you can click on in the Google Apps Control Panel to reset the start page for all users.

Until that happens, however, it's best to design your start page first—get it looking as perfect as you can—and then add the bulk of your new users so they can see the changes.

Winding Down from the Start

In this chapter, you learned how to construct your Google Apps Start Page. You created a customized sub-domain and interacted with the Start Page editor to build a good-looking header and footer. Then, you manipulated some content modules and Google gadgets to help create a full and robust start page experience for your users. In the next chapter, you'll add even more keen communication functionality by embedding blogger and chat functionalities into your Google Apps domain!

8

Buzzing Your Domain Chat and Blogger

In this chapter, you'll add some neat communication features to your Google Apps service. You will examine and then set up the chat features–Google Talk–for your domain, and then you'll add some "value-added" services to your Google Apps setup by blending the blogger into your domain.

Getting into Chatting

You begin your communications tour by logging into your Google Apps Control Panel and looking at the bottom-left corner of the Dashboard, as indicated in Figure 8.1. Click on the Chat link to set up that service for your domain.

Caution
You cannot set up a Google Apps sub-domain for your Google Talk chat. I guess Google wants you to just use a standalone application or use the gadget Web-based version of the program.

Set That Chat!

The Chat Settings page, shown in Figure 8.2, provides you with a link to download Google Talk for Windows. There currently isn't a standalone Google Talk client for Mac–a sad fact in GoogleteerLand to me as a new Apple convert. You can also choose whether you want your users to be able to chat with other Google users outside your domain. You can set up a federated chat network of your own, or you can just disable the ability to chat altogether if you don't want your users to spend their time chatting in your Google Apps Gmail or on the Web.

Figure 8.1
Click on the Google Apps Dashboard Chat link to set up Google Talk for your domain.

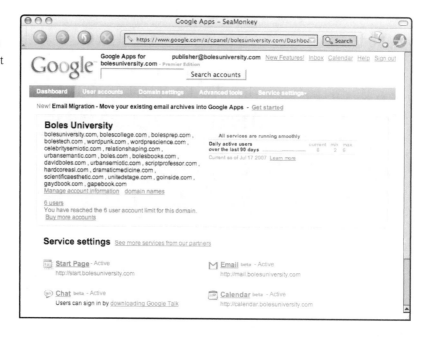

Figure 8.2
Your have a meager few chat setting choices to initialize in your Google Apps Control Panel.

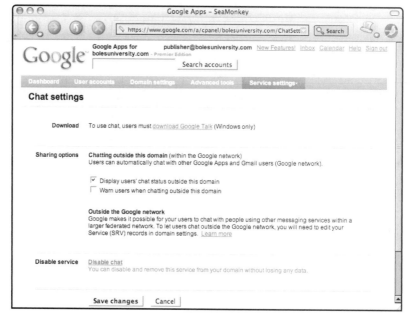

Note
You can make voice calls with the Google Talk Windows client, and you can also drag-and-drop files and folders to your chat mates. You can even continue to chat while the files are being transferred.

Chatting with Other Federated Networks
Say you want to chat with other users who are not using Google Talk or who are not connected to Google Talk through their current chat service. You can, if you are willing and technically savvy, set up your domain to work with other "federated networks" by adding SRV records for your domain.

When you enter the following information, you must replace "gmail.com" with the name of your domain. DO NOT replace "google.com." If you have no idea how to add or edit SRV records, turn your eyes away from the following and turn the page now!

_xmpp-server._tcp.gmail.com. IN SRV 5 0 5269 xmpp-server.l.google.com.

_xmpp-server._tcp.gmail.com. IN SRV 20 0 5269 xmpp-server1.l.google.com.

_xmpp-server._tcp.gmail.com. IN SRV 20 0 5269 xmpp-server2.l.google.com.

_xmpp-server._tcp.gmail.com. IN SRV 20 0 5269 xmpp-server3.l.google.com.

_xmpp-server._tcp.gmail.com. IN SRV 20 0 5269 xmpp-server4.l.google.com.

_jabber._tcp.gmail.com. IN SRV 5 0 5269 xmpp-server.l.google.com.

_jabber._tcp.gmail.com. IN SRV 20 0 5269 xmpp-server1.l.google.com.

_jabber._tcp.gmail.com. IN SRV 20 0 5269 xmpp-server2.l.google.com.

_jabber._tcp.gmail.com. IN SRV 20 0 5269 xmpp-server3.l.google.com.

_jabber._tcp.gmail.com. IN SRV 20 0 5269 xmpp-server4.l.google.com.

Forced into Web and Mail Chatting

Because I am not on a Windows box, I am unable to start a standalone Google Talk chat session. Recall from Chapter 7 that any gadgets you add to your Google Apps Start Page are not visible to existing users. So you're, like, stuck when you want to chat with your users and friends! Luckily, if you remember, you added Google Talk to your Google Apps Web Pages in Chapter 6! You're saved! I can show you the how and why of Google Talk in action with Google Apps. Figure 8.3 shows Google Talk quietly and politely sitting on the Web page we created together, ready to spring into useful action!

Figure 8.3

The Google Talk gadget appears on the page we created together in Chapter 6.

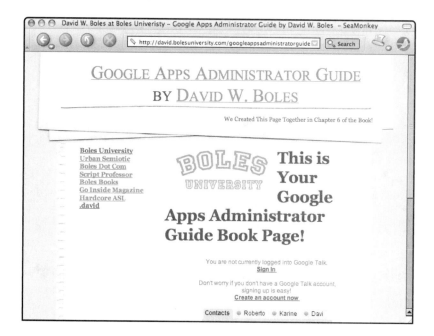

Signing In to Web Chat

Okay, so now I'm signed in to the Google Talk *gadget* (also referred to as a *widget*) on my Google Apps Web page, as you can see in Figure 8.4. I'm not big on chat–I much prefer email communication because I can control the when and the where of the non-real time reply–so my pre-existing chat options are limited. I've heard great things about that "David Boles" fellow, so I'll click on him to see if he's available!

The First Sign of Insanity

As you can see in Figure 8.5, I have found myself, and I am chatting away with my one and only! Is the first sign of insanity engaging yourself in a Google Talk conversation–or is the first sign of madness not realizing you're chatting with yourself in Google Talk?

Inviting Mail Madness

Wait! I'm not done with the madness and parlor tricks! Figure 8.6 shows you how easy it is to log in to your Google Apps Gmail account, click on the Quick Contacts link in the left sidebar, and then choose someone in your contacts list for chatting. Once again, I've found that wonderful Boles boy, so let's see if we can engage him just one more time in the ongoing insanity by clicking on the Chat button found in his contact pop-up window.

Figure 8.4
After you sign in to Google Talk, you are provided with a list of your available contacts for chatting.

Figure 8.5
The first sign of insanity: engaging yourself in a Google Talk chat, enjoying it, and feeling completely entertained at the end.

Tip

If annoying people want to chat with you, you can block them when their request to chat pops up. Blocking them will effectively stop them from seeing your online status without them knowing you did so.

Figure 8.6

You can invite Google Talk chats using your Google Apps Gmail contact list.

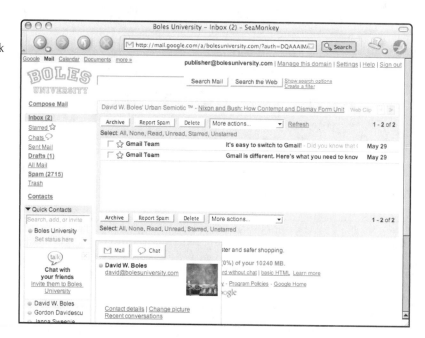

Playing Along with the Crazy Man

In Figure 8.7 I have once again decided to play along with my own crazy antics and accepted an invitation to chat with myself. The idea here is to show you how Google Talk interacts with your Google Apps Gmail setup. You can chat right in your regular Gmail window, or you can click on the pop-out arrow at the bottom of the chat window to get more room for your online chatting.

Mandating Chat Privacy

Your chat history can be saved by default. That means anyone who has access to your account can search your chats and read them. You can turn off that feature, as indicated in Figure 8.8, under your Chat settings in Google Apps Gmail. Even if you want to save your chats, you can always go off the record and not have the conversation logged. If you invoke the Off the Record option, both you and the person you are chatting with on Google Talk will be notified of the change in status. As well, you can manage in your Chat settings how many Quick Contacts you

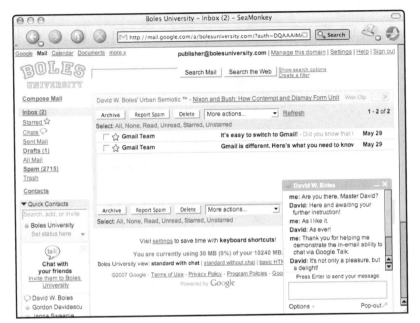

Figure 8.7
It's easy and fun to chat in Gmail with Google Talk.

want to see, where those contacted will be located in your Web view, and whether you want contacts auto-added to your chat list.

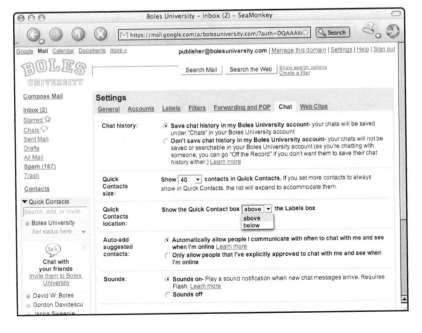

Figure 8.8
You can control individual chat parameters in your Google Apps Gmail Settings area.

> **Caution**
> If you are chatting with someone *not* on the Google Talk network and you go off the record, keep in mind that the person could still be recording every keystroke of your conversation on his end with his chat client. It's best to never disclose anything in any Web chat that would later embarrass you if it were published on the Internet or passed on to other parties.

Blogger in the Google Apps Grassy Knoll

When you add, investigate, and manipulate new features for the Google Apps setup in this book, I always start you off with a shot of the Dashboard in order to orient you and familiarize you with where you are. This section about Blogger and Google Apps is no exception—but it does carry a caveat.

Blogger is Google's blogging product, but it isn't, as of this writing, officially bundled as a part of Google Apps. But, it was once, sort of, as you can see in Figure 8.9. The Blogger logo is prominent and most interestingly situated in the middle of Google Apps Dashboard with a link that says Blogger for Your Domain celebrated with a New! annotation in bright red.

Interesting: Is this a screenshot of the Google Apps Grassy Knoll?

I apologize for the grittiness of the Blogger-included image, but it was provided by the Google Apps Web site in that manner. Although its nonstandard look and feel might seem odd, the importance of sharing the image with you now, instead of just explaining it, was worth it.

Figure 8.9

A mysterious Google Apps Grassy Knoll Blogger For Your Domain link appeared on the official Google Apps Web site in April 2007. It hints at things that never were, but that one day may be.

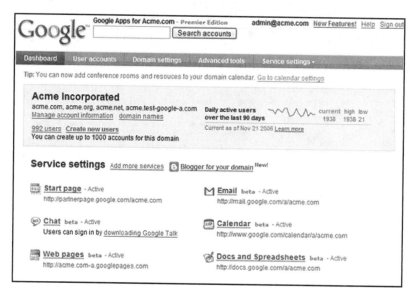

Blogger was never formally embedded into Google Apps, but that image of Blogger in the Google Apps Dashboard was taken directly from the official Google Apps Web site in April 2007. There was, at one time at least, a semipublic plan to implement Blogger into the Google Apps domain, and we all know it will happen soon. Even though that screenshot has since been removed by Google, you can still kludge a way to get Blogger to work with your Google Apps domain. The remainder of this chapter will show you how to do just that.

Bundling Blogger into Google Apps

The first thing you need to do in order to fit Blogger into your domain is make sure you already have a Blogger blog. You must also know what you want your sub-domain to be when all is set up and done. I chose "blog.bolesuniversity.com" because it is easy to remember and because it fits in with the other naming conventions I've created across the rest of my Boles University Google Apps domain. The process of creating a Blogger sub-domain for your Google Apps domain is the same as every other sub-domain you've created. You can get the steps in Chapter 3, using the "ghs.google.com." domain as the redirect for your "blog." CNAME sub-domain.

Blasting Your Blogger Publishing Settings

Once you've set up the CNAME for your Google Apps Blogger blog, log in to Blogger. You need to tell Blogger you are publishing your blog on a custom domain–your Google Apps domain, really. You can find that page in Figure 8.10. Get there by choosing Settings and then Publishing from the Blogger administration area. Enter the URL you want to use for your blog.

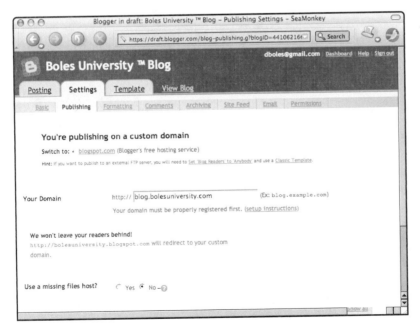

Figure 8.10
Enter the URL you want to use for publishing Blogger on the Web as part of your Google Apps domain.

> **Tip**
> Don't worry about the pre-existing address of your blog if you've been using it for a long time because Blogger will do for you what they did for me: redirect your readers! You can test this yourself with my blog. http://bolesuniversity.blogspot.com will take you directly to http://blog.bolesuniversity.com. Every time a redirect like that happens, I get tingles thinking about the magic of the Internet.

Burning Your Blogger Site Feed

Google recently purchased FeedBurner, which is a fine company that specializes in RSS feed propagation. The reason you'd use a service like FeedBurner is to get a super-detailed and in-depth snapshot of your readers and how they are finding and enjoying you—or not! By using a FeedBurner RSS feed, your blog readers also get a full-featured and pleasant-looking feed away from needing to be connected live on the Web to read your stuff.

Figure 8.11 shows you that Google has already fit FeedBurner into its Blogger Site Feed settings. You only need to enter your post-feed redirect URL into the text box and then click the bright orange Save Settings button on the bottom of the page. You're set to burn! Notice the URL I'm using for my feed? "feeds.bolesuniversity.com/boles" is my RSS feed URL, which was customized in, you guessed it, FeedBurner! I will next show you how to burn your Blogger feed with a custom FeedBurner sub-domain and make it all fit in with Google Apps for your domain.

Figure 8.11
Burning your Blogger feed with a post-feed redirect URL is easy with FeedBurner.

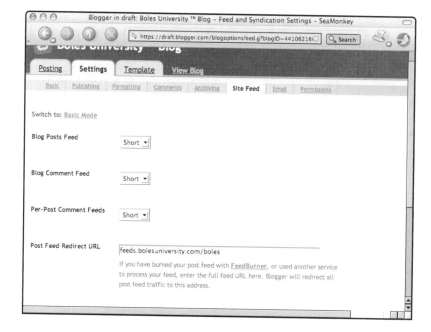

Note
You can use any RSS propagation service to redirect your Blogger post-feed URL in case you aren't using FeedBurner to burn your feeds.

Burning the Boles University Blog

Welcome to the world of FeedBurner! I'm going to take you on a quick tour to show you what Google FeedBurner offers to your Blogger RSS feed. Figure 8.12 shows the main Analyze page for my Boles University blog, as managed in my FeedBurner Dashboard. I expect all of this FeedBurner information to be folded into Google Apps or Blogger in the future, so for now anyway, don't be tossed off by the "feedburner.com" URL you'll see in future images in the rest of this chapter.

I Reburned My Feed and All I Got Were Lost Readers!

The original RSS feed for my Boles University blog was http://blog.bolesuniversity.com/feeds/posts/default.

All my users were using that RSS feed when I changed over to the following URL using the FeedBurner service:

http://feeds.bolesuniversity.com/boles

You may have noticed that I now have only four RSS readers of my blog! Yikes! Where did all my readers go?

My readers are still around, they are just using the original RSS feed address, and that's something you need to keep in mind if you decide to reburn your RSS feed.

Post a notice on your blog that you have a new RSS feed address. Send your readers email announcing the change if you can. Using Blogger and FeedBurner makes it simpler to change your RSS feed address because Blogger does all the dirty work behind the scenes and makes the change seamless for you and your readers.

Keep in mind when you reburn your feed, you will lose those readers who were using that original RSS feed. Don't worry. In time, your readers will discover your new RSS feed. If they don't change to the new RSS address, they will likely lose fresh updates because the old feed will just stop updating with new posts.

The best thing to do is to force the death of your old RSS feed. You can do this by pushing a newly burned RSS address to invisibly replace the old one via a service like FeedBurner.

Figure 8.12
This is the FeedBurner
Dashboard for my Boles
University blog where I
will work to set up my
RSS feed.

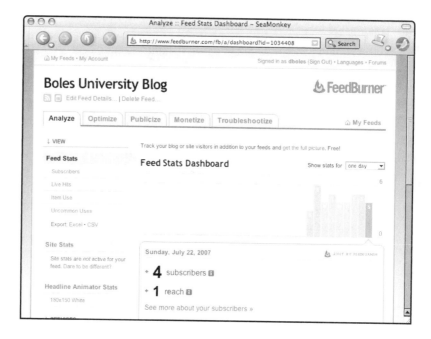

Analyzing the Burn

As you can see in Figure 8.13, FeedBurner has a really clean and efficient workspace. You can modify your feed title, and you will need to know the URL of your original Blogger feed in order to take advantage of FeedBurner's slicker RSS redirect. The following list shows the original feed URLs for my Boles University blog on Blogger. Remember, these URLs don't work any longer because they have been replaced by my FeedBurner feed. I find the third URL–full feed–to be most useful and friendliest to use in all situations:

* http://blog.bolesuniversity.com/atom.xml is Blogger's old ATOM feed.
* http://blog.bolesuniversity.com/rss.xml is Blogger's RSS feed.
* http://blog.bolesuniversity.com/feeds/posts/default is full feed.
* http://blog.bolesuniversity.com/feeds/posts/summary is the summary feed.

Tip
When you set up your FeedBurner account, you will be invited to choose a username and a unique name for your blog. These names will be used in your FeedBurner URL to burn your RSS feed. The name of my Boles University Blogger feed on FeedBurner is "boles" to keep it clean and simple.

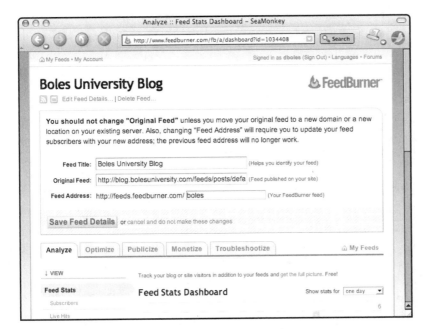

Figure 8.13
Make sure you know the RSS address of your original Blogger feed in order to reburn that feed through FeedBurner.

Rebranding Your Burned Brand

Now it's time to set up your FeedBurner CNAME in order to rebrand your RSS feed using Feed-Burner in concert with your Google Apps domain name. If you need a step-by-step reminder about how to change your DNS zone file to add a CNAME record, please review the instructions in Chapter 3. In Figure 8.14, I chose feeds for my sub-domain, and instead of using the current "ghs.google.com." address, I had to use the specific FeedBurner address of "feeds.feedburner.com." (Don't forget the trailing period!)

> **Caution**
> FeedBurner requires a unique account name that is tied to the feed your want to burn. This account name will then be placed at the end of your rebranded FeedBurner URL. I understand that is confusing; the easiest way to understand the concept is to realize that "feeds.feedburner.com/boles" is "feeds.bolesuniversity.com/boles" even after the CNAME change. You're really just swapping out "feedburner" for "bolesuniversity" in that CNAME change. That might not be enough of a rebranded URL distinction to make it worth your while to modify your DNS zone file.

Figure 8.14
You can swap your domain
name for FeedBurner's in
your rebranded and
reburned RSS feed.

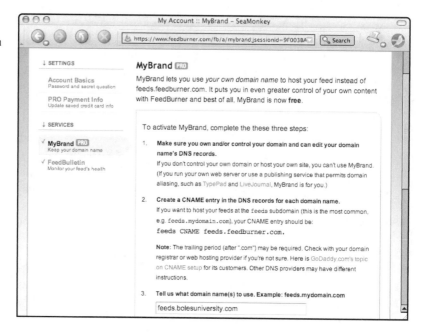

Optimizing the Burned Burn

FeedBurner offers you lots of keen ways to optimize your RSS feed, and I will leave those delights for you to discover. I do appreciate the clean look of the FeedBurner feed, as witnessed in Figure 8.15. Be sure to check the Your Feed area on the Optimize tab to make sure FeedBurner is seeing and propagating the right feed.

Calling All FeedMedics, STAT!

Another great feature FeedBurner offers is FeedMedic, as shown in Figure 8.16. FeedMedic diligently watches your RSS for problems. If there are any problems reading your feed, you get an email warning you to fix the problem. You can also get FeedMedic alerts via a private RSS feed just for you. As "luck" would have it, my Blogger feed was acting completely wacky over the weekend I was writing this chapter, which allowed me to show you just what a FeedMedic alert looks like. Google was obviously working on the Blogger back end, perhaps integrating FeedBurner directly into Google Apps. You can typically go for months without getting any sort of FeedMedic trouble reports.

Figure 8.15
Even the unstyled view of the FeedBurner RSS feed has a clean and eminently viewable look and feel.

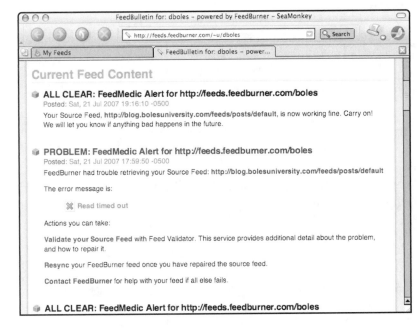

Figure 8.16
FeedMedic alerts you to the illness of your originating RSS feed before it reburns it.

Animating Your Burned Feed

Once your feed is rebranded with your domain and reburned via FeedBurner, you can publicize your blog feed in many ways. The Headline Animator is a fine piece of programming that takes your RSS feed headlines and places them in a convenient subscription box; you can see an example in Figure 8.17. That 180 pixel by 150 pixel box can be placed on any Web page so that readers can see your writing better. You can also design your own link choices and even choose from a variety of styles and banner sizes.

Figure 8.17

Created a Headline Animator to publicize your RSS feed on your Web pages.

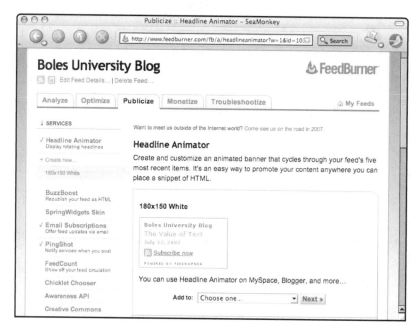

Adding RSS Animation to Blogger

When you have an animated RSS headline ready to insert into a Web page or a blog, you can choose to directly add the animator to your Blogger blog by clicking the Add to Blogger button, as indicated in Figure 8.18.

> **Note**
> FeedBurner currently works with MySpace, Blogger, and TypePad for optimizing and publicizing your feed. Will that openness between competing information resources remain in the future? Only Google knows for sure, so you need to make sure you create smart choices for the longevity of your blog and RSS feed when you use FeedBurner to reburn your non-Blogger–hosted blog.

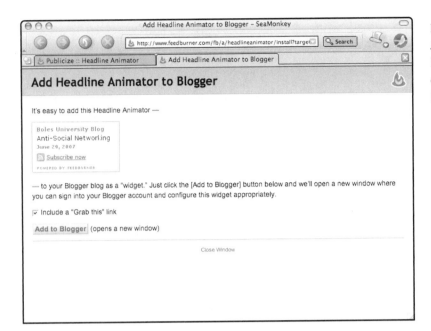

Figure 8.18
Adding your animated headline to Blogger is as easy as clicking on a button.

Back to Burning with Blogger

When you click on the Add to Blogger button, you go from FeedBurner directly into your Blogger setup. Figure 8.19 demonstrates the Add Page Element page, where FeedBurner takes you to add your FeedBurner gadget to Blogger. When you're ready to add the element, click the Add Widget button. Your headline animator will be added to your blog template.

> **Tip**
> You may wonder why would you bother adding a headline animator if you already have your Blogger RSS feed invisibly churning through a FeedBurner reburn. The answer is that repetition wins minds and reinforces memes. Offering a multiplicity of ways to add your blog to someone else's life is valuable and important if you want to be widely, regularly, and reliably read.

Checking Your Blogger Template

Once you add the Headline Animator gadget, as shown in Figure 8.20, Blogger presents you with a template interface, where you can check the placement of your gadget compared with other page elements. By default, the gadget becomes the first choice in the left column. You will get an announcement that your headline animator was successfully added. Click the Save button to keep the gadget in place and add it live to your blog.

Figure 8.19
Now that you're back in Blogger, you need to click the Add Widget button to add your FeedBurner Headline Animator to your blog.

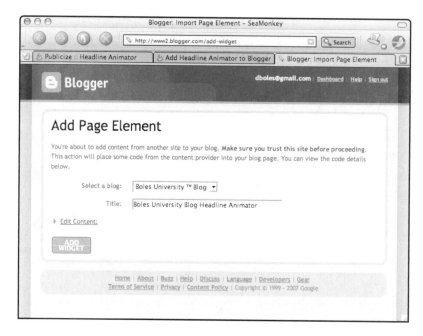

Figure 8.20
The Headline Animator is added to your Blogger template.

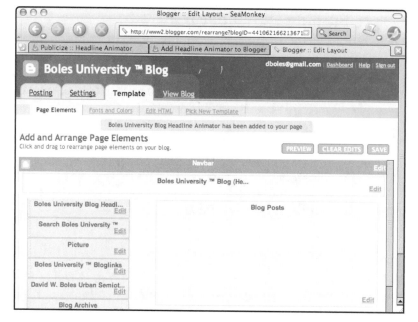

Confirming the Live Feed

As you know by now, trust everyone but not every technology, so you need to make sure your new headline gadget is actively added and working. Figure 8.21 shows a live shot of my Boles University blog; you can see my shiny new FeedBurner Headline Animator smiling back from the left sidebar.

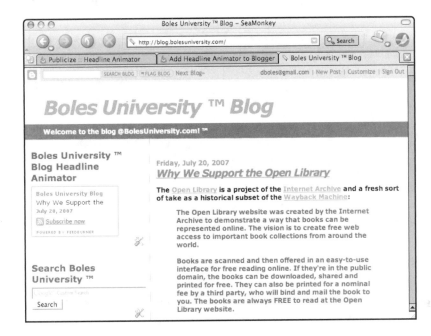

Figure 8.21

Here's how the Headline Animator looks in the Boles University blog.

Creative Reburning

If you are feeling wily, and you are comfortable working with raw HTML, you can copy and paste your FeedBurner animated headline and add it to any Web page or blog. In Figure 8.22, you can see how I added it to my Urban Semiotic blog at http://UrbanSemiotic.com in order to bring my Urban Semiotic readers over and into my Boles University blog! That sort of shared-interest cross-promotion of dreams and intentions is what makes great and valuable interconnections on the Internet.

Figure 8.22

There's my Boles
University RSS Headline
Animator in the sidebar of
my Urban Semiotic blog!
That's cross-promotion at
its best!

Burning Down

In this chapter, you worked on a couple of keen ways to add communication value to your
Google Apps domain. You learned how to set up and enable Google Talk on your Web site and
in Gmail. You also discovered the value of RSS feeds and using FeedBurner. You learned how
to integrate it all with Blogger in your Google Apps domain setup, even though Blogger and
FeedBurner aren't officially–as of the writing of this chapter–embedded into Google Apps
proper, yet. In Chapter 9, you'll discover the power and beauty of Google Docs!

9 Creating Your Domain Docs

Google Apps Docs and Spreadsheets might soon be known as "Google Docs and Spreadsheets and Presentations." Or, perhaps just "Google Docs" or perhaps something else altogether because, you see, as I write this chapter, rumors are still wildly rampant that the announcement Google made many months ago on the Official Google Blog–located at http://googleblog.blogspot.com–might finally be happening with the addition of a PowerPoint-like addition to Google Docs and Spreadsheets known in the online rumor mill for now as Presentations.

This chapter does not include Presentations coverage, and that's okay because Presentations will only add functionality and not change how Google Docs works. The online bonus chapters (see Chapter 10 for more info) will provide you with the most up-to-date information on any new additions, including Presentations, to Google Docs.

I also understand Google Docs and Spreadsheets will become known simply as Google Docs when the Presentations module is added. Therefore, for now, I refer to the entire suite as Google Docs. This chapter mainly focuses on Google Docs. The Spreadsheets and Presentations modules share the same basic administrative settings, sharing needs, and collaborative features with Docs. I also don't cover every feature of the suite; that would require an entire book itself!

Tip

As of the writing of this book, Google Docs has the following limits: Each document can be up to 500K in file size, plus up to 2MB per embedded image. Each user is limited to 5,000 documents and 5,000 images. These limits might change in the future, so keep an eye on your Google Apps Control Panel for any new features and updates, and you can always use this URL to get the latest updates for storage restrictions: http://www.google.com/support/writely/bin/answer.py?answer=37603.

What's Up, Docs?

You first need to log in to the Google Apps Control Panel and make sure you have Google Docs working right in the Google Apps setup. Notice in the middle of the screen in Figure 9.1 that the Daily Active Users graph is missing again, with a textual "Stay Tuned" in the place of my red and green dynamic graph. That's all part of the Google experience; if you logged out and came back, the graph would likely be there. Click on the Docs and Spreadsheets link on the bottom-right side of the page to move into the special settings screen.

> **Note**
>
> Don't let the "beta" identifiers marked near most of the services scare you while you set up and work with Google Apps. The programs are thoroughly tested, and they work pretty well. Google made its name with products in a perpetual beta state. Even though many of its products have a "beta" label, you won't likely find many programs out on the market that are better than Google's beta products.

Figure 9.1

Your Google Apps Dashboard view gives you a link for setting up Google Docs for your domain.

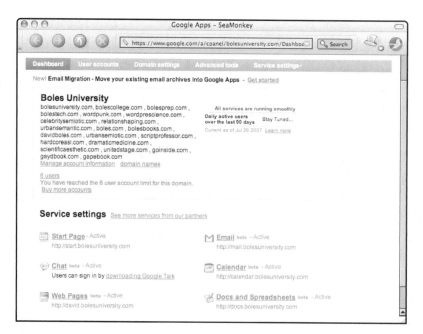

Setting That Sheet!

Here you are again, as indicated in Figure 9.2, in the familiar Service Settings area of the Google Apps Control Panel. This time, you will set up the Docs and Spreadsheets service. If you want to create a sub-domain such as, say "docs.bolesuniversity.com," or something similar that better fits your needs, you can set up your CNAME information via the Change URL link on this page. For a more detailed process describing how to change your DNS zone file to add or modify CNAME entries, please refer to Chapter 3. Another critical decision you need to make while you work on this page is whether you want to share your documents outside of your domain.

As a self-confessed control freak and sometime paranoid, I will always choose the security of privacy and nonsharing over the possibility of inadvertently "sharing" something on the Web. I understand that restricting sharing to domain users only makes it hard to collaborate outside your domain, but that's a tradeoff I am willing to pay for and abide by in order to maintain a secure workspace. So think hard about your Docs and Spreadsheets as you set your sharing options. Here are your options:

* You can choose not to share outside your domain but allow your domain users to receive Google Docs from the outside world.

* You can let users share Docs and Spreadsheets outside your domain with a warning— although I'm uncertain what good that warning would serve.

* You can just give in and let everything be shared and found online.

* You can also turn on and disable your Google Apps Docs on this page.

Don't forget to click the Save Changes button when you're satisfied with your selections.

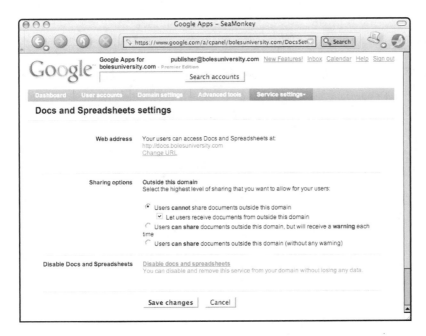

Figure 9.2
You can create universal settings for your Google Docs from this Service Settings page.

Security Is an Imperative, But It Should Not Suffocate

Security is important, but don't let concerns over security push you away from successfully collaborating with others.

If there are people outside your domain whom you really need to work with, but you are a super-smart administrator so you do not allow sharing beyond your domain, you can simply make these users part of your domain!

Yes, go ahead and make those "outsiders" members of your domain!

Give those you want to collaborate with an account. If you have Google Apps Premier Edition, it'll cost you about $50.00 USD a year for a single account. BUY THEM AN ACCOUNT!

Is it worth $50 a year in order to retain your security and privacy in the work process? Yes, of course it is!

I recommend this method because it makes everyone involved in the process secure and accountable for their work.

Logging In to Load Up

Now let's head over into our login page of the Google Apps Docs program by using "docs.bolesuniversity.com" as the URL. As you can see in Figure 9.3, that pretty URL changed to a big ugly URL, but because that ugly URL is secure via HTTPS, don't let it bother you much. I know you know I love these Google Apps login screens because you get updated tidbits of

Figure 9.3

You can directly log in to your Google Docs page from this screen after setting up the sharing options in the Google Apps Control Panel.

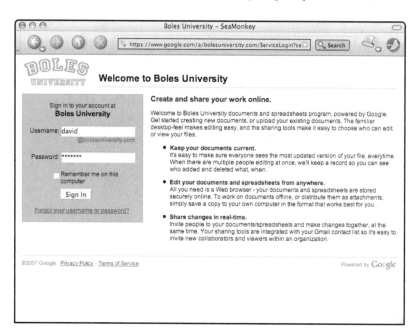

information directly from Google about what's new and improved. It's a great way to get "News of the Day" from Google Apps.

A New Look at Google Docs

Allow me a moment to rant.

Google recently updated the look and feel of their Google Docs workspace, and frankly, I'm not a fan of it. You can see an example in Figure 9.4. I like my screen space to myself, and the giant blue bar in the middle of the screen is disconcerting. It looks very Microsoft Vista-like and, to my eye, incredibly unGoogle-like! You can also see instead of labels that Google Docs now includes—believe it or not—folders! I thought the whole idea behind Google's revolution of the Web was not to compartmentalize in "folders," but instead to combine all information into one giant pool with pointers to related information.

For me, this new design of Google Docs is off-putting and disappointing, but Google did lots of end-user testing, and because we live in a Windows World, I guess Google decided to pretty up their Docs interface by making it look more Microsoft-like. If history is a guide, we might soon see this design as a part of Gmail. My, that will be a dark day on the Internet for all the geeks and miscreants we know, love, and yearn to become!

Okay, rant over.

Google Docs provides lots of information in the left sidebar. You can choose from three views: Created By Me, Starred, and Trash. You can also easily create and manage folders and view documents by type—either Document or Spreadsheet. You also have a quick view of your current collaborators.

The main document view provides timeline indicators of all your current documents.

Tip

You can now sort your documents by clicking on column headers, and you can hide or archive documents you don't need to see listed every day. Just click the checkbox next to the file and then click the Hide button on your toolbar to remove the document from your active list. You can unhide your documents by reversing the process—click on the Hide icon in the sidebar and dragging the documents into your active view list. Don't forget you can also use the Search Documents button at the top of the main Google Docs view. It allows you to move easily and cogently through your mass of documents to quickly find what you want.

Figure 9.4
Welcome to the new look
and feel of the Google
Docs workspace!

Settings with Styles

Now let's click on the Settings link in the upper-right corner of the Google Docs interface so you can make all the features work as you desire. You don't have a lot of options you can set, but we should still investigate their possibilities together.

Missing Docs

Figure 9.5 shows the Google Docs General settings. You can pick a language and your preferred time zone and, quite encouragingly, whether you want a right-to-left interaction when you write. You can also import other documents from pre-existing Gmail accounts, from other accounts on your domain, or from another domain that allows public sharing. This is a welcome and delightful feature that instantly draws all your eligible old public documents into your new Google Apps Docs workspace.

> **Note**
> You can also upload existing documents from your local computer by using the Upload button on the giant blue bar in the main Google Docs view.

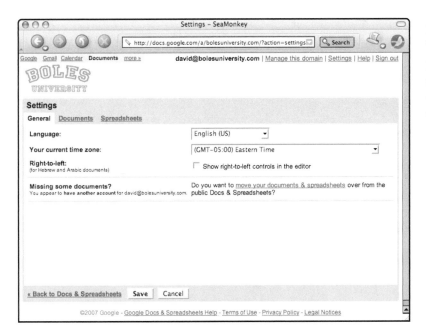

Figure 9.5
The General Settings area provides a way to pull your old public documents into the new Google Apps Docs workspace.

What's in a Name?

Clicking on the Documents Settings tab provides you with the sad little screen in Figure 9.6. You can only type in the display name. Why aren't there more features here to manipulate and control? Will the impending Presentations upgrade offer users some more exciting features? Only Google knows!

A Name Is Better than Nothing!

I didn't think a Settings screen could get lonelier than the one you just saw for Documents, but the Settings screen for Spreadsheets in Figure 9.7 speaks a great and lonesome sadness. It wins the title for the most unsettable setting in all of Google Apps: "There are currently no settings for spreadsheets."

> **Tip**
> Dry your eyes. The fact that a page exists for Spreadsheets settings hints, nay indicates, that there will be some settings at some point, right? Why would Google create a Spreadsheets link to nowhere unless it planned to add settings at some point? You might even be able to access those settings right now, in your updated version of Google Docs!

Figure 9.6
A sad Documents Settings interface: type in your name.

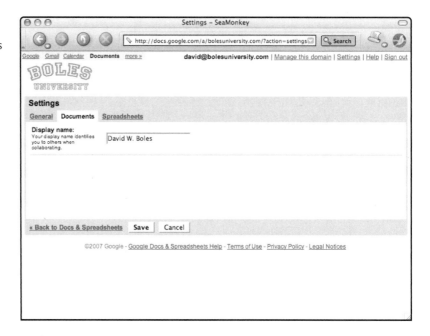

Figure 9.7
The loneliest setting: The Google Docs Spreadsheets Settings allows you to set nothing at all. But check Google online for updates!

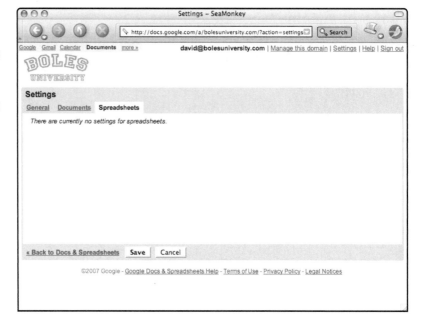

Back to Building

Enough of the lonely settings! Let's head back into the main Google Docs interface. Click on the Share tab on the right side of your screen. You are presented with the interface you see in Figure 9.8. Let's collaborate on a Google Docs Rule Writing on the Web! document. Click on the Invite Collaborators button to begin the invitation process.

> **Note**
> You can also choose to invite people to view your document only, without giving them the right to change your document as a collaborator.

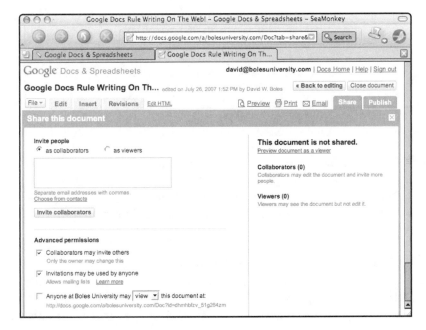

Figure 9.8
If you want others to collaborate on your document, you need to share it first.

Choosing Collaborators

After you click on the Invite Collaborators button, the Contacts Chooser will pop up. This might look familiar from the Calendar invitation system used in Chapter 5, and it pretty much is the same process for inviting people to work on a document with you. Highlight the collaborators you want onboard. After you do so, a green checkmark will appear next to their names. I'm inviting myself again so I can show you how the collaborative process works with Google Apps Docs. When you're finished inviting your collaborators, click on the Done button to move to the next step.

Figure 9.9
Highlight the collaborators you want to invite to work on a document.

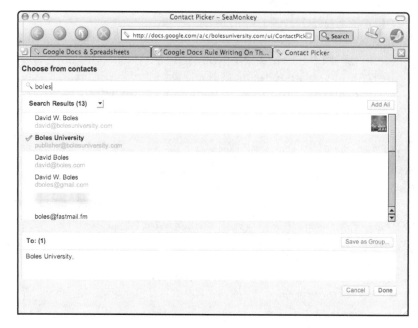

Sending Invitations

It isn't enough to just invite the collaborators; you should also fulfill the next step in the chain and tell your collaborators about the document, as Google Docs offers in Figure 9.10. You can be specific about your needs and expectations. You can skip the invitation step, but if you choose to be formal with your invite, click the Send button to scoot your invite into the Google cloud.

Accepting the Collaboration Invitation Challenge

In Figure 9.11, you can see the collaboration invitation I sent myself to invite myself to work on a document. I am thrilled to be included! The quickest way to get started is to follow the instruction in the email invite and click on the enclosed document URL provided in the message.

Caution

If you choose to skip the invitation process, your collaborators will know you've given them access to new documents only if you tell them or if they happen to log in to Google Apps Docs and see the new shared file sitting there waiting for their feedback. If time is of the essence, use the email invitation to immediately let all your collaborators know they have access to your document so they can begin collaborating with you.

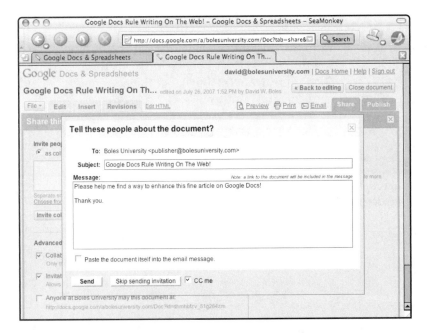

Figure 9.10
A formal invitation to collaborate allows you to set expectations.

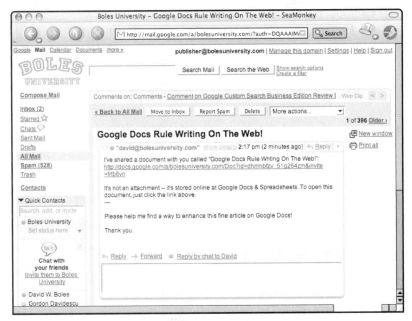

Figure 9.11
Click on the Google Docs URL in your email invite to get started.

Live Docs Collaboration

Okay, so you clicked on the URL provided in the invitation. Google zooms you right into the open edit screen (shown in Figure 9.12) of the Google Docs Rule Writing On The Web! document. You can see there's already some text there. Note the big bar at the bottom-left side of the screen, which shows the other active editors currently online.

Figure 9.12

Collaborating is easy and fun. Just start typing and see who responds!

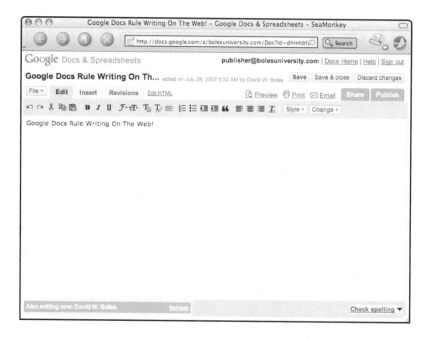

Who Do You Think You Are?

One of the pitfalls, of course, in writing online in a collaborative effort with others is that you have to consider and incorporate their feedback. Figure 9.13 provides a commentary from me on one of my own sentences. When I was in my other Google Apps account, I clicked on the Insert tab and then chose the Comments link to provide my question about the meaning of a *meme.* That comment immediately appears in the write window on my Publisher Google Apps account.

Head Down, Grindstone on Nose

As you can see in Figure 9.14, I decided to take my own advice and define meme for the readers. It's a great word, but few people realize its genesis or real meaning. Most folks think a meme is a list of silly things they've done in their lives that they then publish on their blogs. I just kept typing, nose still on grindstone, and the new paragraph was inserted after the comment.

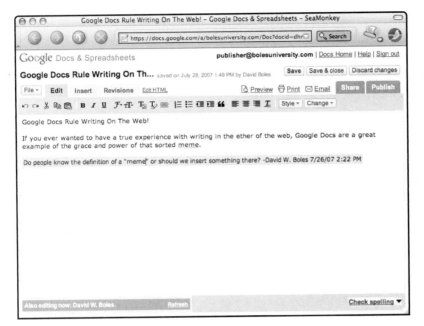

Figure 9.13
You can give instant
feedback by inserting
comments into
documents.

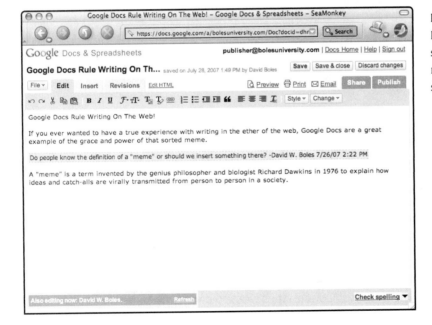

Figure 9.14
Document comments
serve as reminders,
notations, and thoughts
shared with others.

Tip

You can also place a comment on an article you are actively writing by choosing the Insert tab and then the Comment link. This allows you to write a note to yourself or place an alert on a paragraph for others to understand your thinking process.

You Changed What? PUT IT BACK!

One of the best and most powerful features of Google Apps Docs is the ongoing ability to check the revisions of a document across the arc of its life. When you click on the Revisions tab, a list of all the revisions and when they were made appears, as shown in Figure 9.15. You then have the power to compare one revision against another. This list shows you who made what changes when. You can revert back to an older edit if you don't like the changes that were made after your initial work was done. Once you have selected the revisions you want to compare, click the Compare Checked button to see the changes.

Figure 9.15
Compare Checked is a powerful way to compare different revisions of a single document.

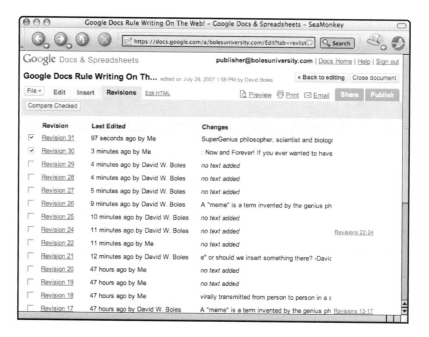

I'll Show You Mine if You Show Me Yours

Figure 9.16 demonstrates the power of Google Apps Docs to compare revisions over time. In this view I am looking at the differences between revisions 30 and 31. Changes are color coded based on author, which makes it super simple to see who did what and when. When you're finished comparing, click on the Back to Editing button in the upper-right side of your screen.

Caution

Be aware that there's no hiding from responsibility in the editorial process in Google Apps Docs. Be kind and supportive in the suggestions and changes you make. If someone else messes with your stuff in a mean or inappropriate way, you can see it right there in your revision comparisons. Then you can have your revenge!

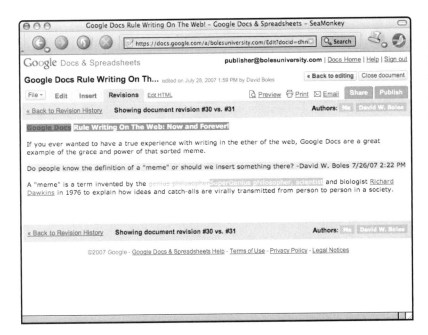

Figure 9.16
Google Apps Docs visually links and demonstrates the changes made to documents with color and name attributions.

Eating More Raw HTML

If you are creating a Web document—and by default all Google Apps Docs begin as HTML files unless and until you save them in a different file format—you can click on the Edit HTML link to get a gander at the raw HTML Google created for you, as indicated in Figure 9.17. You can futz with the code if there's something you don't like and need to edit, or you can just click on the Back to Editing the Document link and head back into the general edit view.

Figure 9.17
Raw HTML editing gives you a powerful means of control over the look and feel of your Web documents.

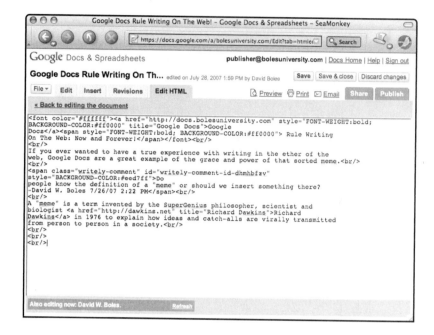

Pubbing Your Docs

It's always a thrill to publish a document because it gives your words and thoughts more power. When you're ready to go live, click on the Publish tab on the right side of your screen. Figure 9.18 shows the Publish view. Google reminds you that the document will only be available in your domain and not beyond. If you make changes to the document, you can click on the Re-publish Document button to update the changed view, or if you don't want your document to be read by others, you can click the Stop Publishing button to make your document private again. If you check the Automatically Re-Publish when Changes Are Made button, Google will always provide the freshest and most up-to-date view of the document in its published view.

Blogging with Google Docs

If you choose to make your documents public in the Google Apps Control Panel, you can also publish your documents on the Web as a blog entry using the Post to Blog option! You cannot post documents to your blog using Google Docs if you do not choose the administrative setting to share documents outside of your domain.

Yes, you can use Google Docs as a rough blogging client for many of the most popular blog platforms like WordPress, Blogger, LiveJournal, and many others.

You will need to provide your login information, such as username, password, and any other special settings that Google Docs will need to know to gain publishing access to the backend of your blog.

You can even use Google Docs to post blog articles on a self-hosted blogging site as long as you have server-side permissions to post updates from afar. Don't forget to click on the Test button after you enter your information to confirm all your settings were properly entered and are working right.

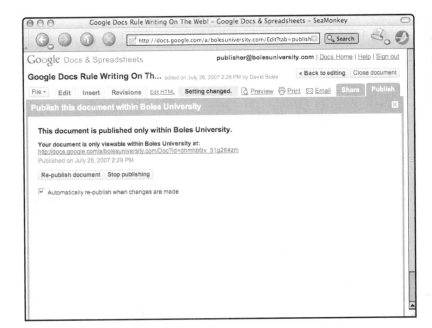

Figure 9.18
When your collaboration is over, your team can publish the document for public viewing.

Saving Your Docs As

Another powerful feature of Google Apps Docs is how it's updated frequently with more and more ways to save a document. If you click on the File button, a menu will drop down, as demonstrated in Figure 9.19. You can see all the options for saving files: as HTML, RTF, a Word document, an OpenOffice document, a PDF, or plain text. That list is often updated with new file formats, so keep an eye on the File menu. If you look farther down the menu, you will see a Document Settings link. It looks a little out of place there, but clicking on it will take you to an interesting, if hidden, options screen.

Finding the Hidden Docs Settings

The Document Settings screen seen in Figure 9.20 provides a powerful, yet hidden, way to modify your document. You can set hard, universal, settings here for all your documents or for just the document you are currently editing. Even though Google Docs officially doesn't support

Figure 9.19
You have lots of Save As options for your Google Apps document files.

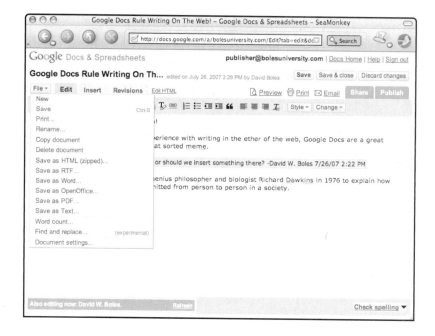

Figure 9.20
You can set specific document settings on this Google Apps Docs preferences screen.

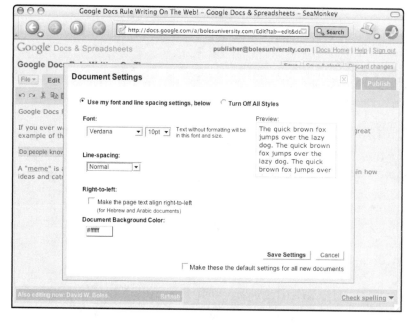

templates, you can quite easily see how this hidden feature could serve as a sort of documents template. Be certain to click the Save Settings button if you make any changes.

Spreadsheets?

Okay, it's time now to take a look at how spreadsheets work in Google Docs for your domain. Choose New from the File menu and select Spreadsheets from the menu to start working on a new Spreadsheets file.

> **Note**
> As of the writing of this book, each spreadsheet can be up to 10,000 rows, 256 columns, 100,000 cells, or 40 sheets–whichever of those limits is reached first. Each user is limited to 1,000 spreadsheets. Eleven spreadsheets can be open at once. You can import spreadsheets up to 1MB each in the following formats: XLS, CSV, DOS, TXT, TSV, and TSB.

We Don't Need No Stinkin' Spreadsheets!

Gak! As you can see in Figure 9.21, Google is not feeling well at the moment. This sort of "wait, I'm not ready!" error messages from the Google Apps server are reminders that you are not working at home and saving to your local computer. You're "out there" in the Google cloud, which means that sometimes you have to wait for Google to be ready to work for you. When I get these sort of hard, dead-in-the-water, error messages from Google, I stop what I'm doing and take a 10-minute break to brush it off. Usually I am able to resume what I was doing before the Google error page smacked me betwixt the eyes.

Skipping the Spread

Because sharing and collaborating on a spreadsheet aren't different from sharing and collaborating on a document under the Google Docs banner, I won't dig into spreadsheets in this book. All the interactive ideals are the same in spreadsheets; the only aspect that changes is the type of information being shared.

> **Tip**
> You can *discuss* (have a live chat) with your collaborators while working online with a spreadsheet. The Discuss tab is found on the right side of your Edit view next to the Share and Publish tabs, and after you invite your collaborators to attend, you can chat away in real time as you edit the spreadsheet.

Figure 9.21

Gak! Google burped! You can't create a Spreadsheets file right now! When you get this error message, come back in 10 minutes; 30 seconds is typically too optimistic.

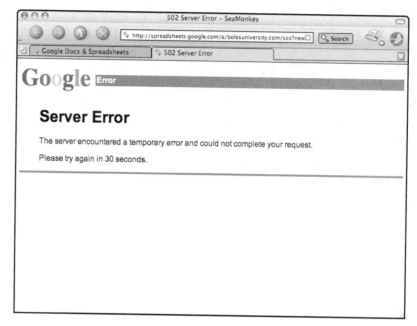

Using Google Spreadsheets for Project Management

Google Docs Spreadsheets does have one peculiar function that you might enjoy. You can turn Spreadsheets into a pseudo-project management platform for all your collaborators.

Here how it's done.

Create a new Google Apps spreadsheet and send out an invite to collaborate on it.

Create these five columns:

* Deadlines

* Missions

* Lead

* Updates

* To Do

Once you share the spreadsheet (or provide a public URL for sharing if your domain setup allows for outside editing and viewing), you can all work together and set deadlines, define individual missions inside the project, take the lead, provide updates, and create to-do lists for each other.

When you're collaborating with others in real time, you can see where they are in the spreadsheet because the cell in which they are working is bordered in their unique color.

Rounding Off the Docs

In this chapter, you discovered the deep collaborative powers of Google Apps Docs for your domain. You learned how to share–or block–documents beyond your domain. You also discovered the power of collaboration and the dangers in making private documents public. You also enjoyed the surprise victory of Google adding new features and programs. In the next chapter, you'll look at where you've been and how far you've come in your discovery of Google Apps, and you will hear about what I hope to see next from Google Apps.

10 The Invisible Chapter of Things to Come

We've come to the end of our *Google Apps Administrator Guide* journey together, and it has been my sheer delight and honor to take this trip with you. You are now as much an expert as I am in manipulating the Google Apps backend through your Control Panel and Dashboard. You now know what I know about how to best work with your users, collaborate with them online, and tend to their needs and issues. You are now free to revise your Google Apps Web Pages and to design your Google Apps Start Page to continue the ongoing journey of life, work, and play, all of which cojoins on the Web to construct who we are and who we will be in the future.

Over the course of *Google Apps Administrator Guide,* you've seen how quickly Google changes things for the betterment of Google Apps. Some of the screenshots you see in this book might not look exactly the same in your home screen. That's okay, and that's by design. I want you to "see and live" in Google Apps just by holding this book in your hands. You don't need to be in front of a computer screen to learn from this book in real time. The intent of this book is to show you semiotically, with images, precisely how Google Apps works. By giving you full screenshots, my goal is to make sure you can orient yourself in place and time based on what you see here and what you're seeing there.

Tending BolesBooks.com for Freshness

The main Web site for *Google Apps Administrator Guide* is located online at http://BolesBooks.com/thomson/, and you can always find the latest information on the book at that site, as indicated in Figure 10.1. Because Google Apps is always in flux, I have decided to protect your purchase of this book with online updates and bonus chapters that will include any and all major changes to Google Apps that occur between the time I finish writing the book and the time the book hits the bookstores. Visiting http://BolesBooks.com/thomson/ often will ensure you always have the latest Google Apps information.

Figure 10.1
http://BolesBooks.com/thomson/ is the homepage for *Google Apps Administrator Guide.*

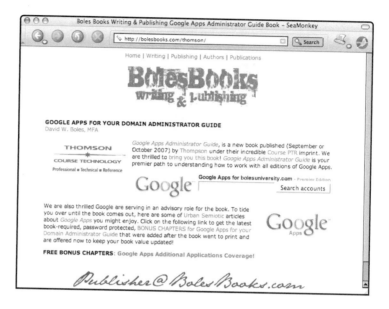

Google Apps Administrator Guide **Bonus Chapters!**

The online bonus chapters for *Google Apps Administrator Guide* are available only to those who purchased this book. You need a username and password to ensure that only those who bought *Google Apps Administrator Guide* can access the updated information and bonus chapters. Check online at http://BolesBooks.com/thomson/ for simple instructions on accessing the protected content. As a formal teaser, you can see in Figure 10.2 the placeholder page for the *Google Apps Administrator Guide* bonus chapters and online updates. That page will soon be password protected, so take a good look at it now if you're only browsing this book and wondering if you want to buy it or not!

Google Apps in the Tomorrow

As you conclude your *Google Apps Administrator Guide* journey, I want to share some final wonderings with you. In May 2007, Google sent out a giant online survey to all current Google Apps users asking for specific and detailed feedback. At the end of the survey, Google asked for a visionary statement on where you hoped Google Apps would end up in the future. I share with you now my response to that Google request.

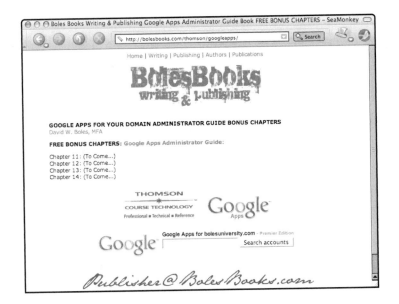

Figure 10.2

This is the password-protected page for the online updates and bonus chapters for *Google Apps Administrator Guide!*

What I Want from Google Apps:

I want everything in a single pool—folders are to labels as separate links are to a congealed Wiki dipping, where everything I want to do is on a solitary sheet—there is no separation or spatiality or links to applications trying to fit into the fuzzy whole of the Apps mentality. If I think it, I want it—without clicking—and that includes Blogger, virtual storage, phone calls, television, radio, history books, live access to future geniuses, and so on...

—May 17, 2007

I have no idea if any of that has meaning to Google, but I do think it provides a prescient path into the way we will all be living online together—with or without Google—and the easiest way to pave that road is through the avenue of exploitation and expression that Google Apps already provides.

See You Soon!

I once again thank you for your interest in *Google Apps Administrator Guide.* If you have some thoughts you'd like to share—I regret I will not be able to provide any technical support for Google Apps—feel free to use any of my email addresses peppered throughout this book for contact. If you decide to touch in with me, please use "*Google Apps Administrator Guide* Inquiry" in the subject of your email message so I will know how you found me, and I can give you my rapt attention! You may also find lots of good links and information online at http://BolesUniversity.com and http://BolesBooks.com.

Take care and be well. I will find your eye again online!

INDEX